Beautiful Sunday

NAME Sara Soliman

SCHOOL Choueifat

CLASS 7ᵗʰ E

SUBJECT Social Studies

DISCOVERING GEOGRAPHY

Settlements

DISCOVERING GEOGRAPHY

Settlements

Tony Ghaye
Senior Lecturer in Teaching Studies,
Worcester College of Higher Education

Lynda Ghaye

Macmillan Education

First published 1983
Reprinted 1985

Published by
MACMILLAN EDUCATION LTD
Houndmills, Basingstoke, Hampshire RG21 2XS
and London
Companies and representatives
throughout the world

Printed in Hong Kong

British Library Cataloguing in Publication Data
Ghaye, Tony
Settlements.–(Discovering geography)
1. Anthropo-geography
I. Title II. Ghaye, Lynda III. Series
307   GF101
ISBN 0–333–28401–1

Preface

This is one of a series of three books intended primarily for use in the first three years of the secondary school. Each book examines a major theme (Settlement, Man and Resources) and does so within a clear framework based on five central geographical concepts (scale, location, association, interaction and change). The books have been written to allow different expressions of each concept to be explored in a variety of contexts. To assist the teacher, the organisation of the material is shown in the list of Contents (page vi). The aim throughout is to confront pupils with real-world issues and to encourage them to present their own knowledge, as well as receive knowledge, in a wide range of forms. Numerous opportunities are offered to extend the activities in each book and to apply them locally.

In order to ensure that the books work in mixed ability classes, the chapters in each book begin in a simple way. The exemplar materials and activities here are designed to motivate and inspire self-confidence. As each chapter progresses it becomes more complex both in terms of language and in the nature of the geographical problems presented to the pupil.

The challenge of assessing these problems, of forming judgements and attitudes and of identifying solutions to them, encourages children to develop an awareness of their own capabilities and an understanding of the world about them. By offering a variety of opportunities to 'learn how to learn' the series will give children the chance to think like geographers.

Contents

1 The Nature of Settlements

2 A Look inside Settlements

1 The nature of settlements

Dwellings

People live in dwellings. These dwellings can vary in their size and shape. They can be built of different materials and vary in age. Some dwellings are mobile. This means they can move around. Other dwellings are not mobile. They stay in the same place for many years.

1 Look at Fig. 1.1. Give each type of dwelling a name.

2 Describe their different sizes and shapes.

3 Make a list of the main materials that have been used to make each type of dwelling.

4 Which are the mobile and non-mobile dwellings?

5 If a settlement has all mobile dwellings it may be there one day and gone the next. Think of an example of this type of settlement.

Fig. 1.1

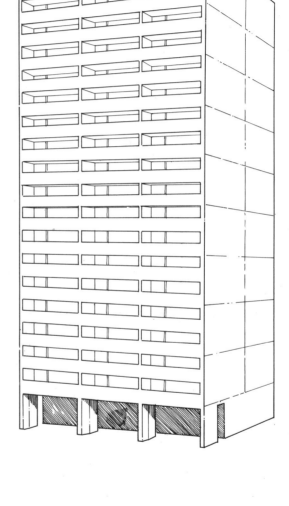

1

Fig. 1.2 (*Above*) An underground dwelling in Coober Pedy, South Australia. (*Below*) A dwelling in Ujung Pandang, Sulawesi

2

Not all dwellings are built on the ground. Some may float on water, some may be built underground, others raised into the air.

6 Look at Fig. 1.2. Why do you think these dwellings have been built in this way?

A settlement usually has other buildings as well as dwellings. These buildings may be places where people can shop, work, play, learn or worship.

7 Look at Fig. 1.3. In which buildings can you do each of these things?
8 Name buildings in your own settlement where you can do each of these things.

All settlements are different

No two settlements are exactly alike. They are different in many ways. Settlements differ in the number of people that live in them. They also differ in the amount of land they cover and in their shape. As settlements satisfy a range of human needs they may have different types and numbers of shops and other functions.

1 How big is your settlement? One way to answer this question is to find out how many people live in it. Try to find out how many people live in your settlement. Table 1.1 gives the total population for four different settlements in West Sussex. Draw and label a histogram (bar graph) to show that settlements vary in their size. Each settlement has a different total population.

Table 1.1

Settlement	Total population in 1976
1 Horsham	27 000
2 Burgess Hill	20 000
3 Southwater	13 000
4 Billingshurst	5 000

Settlement sprawl

Some very big settlements are called conurbations. They are made up of many smaller settlements and are vast areas of urban land use. Greater London is a conurbation. It is made up of smaller settlements like Enfield, Richmond and Harrow. Nine million people live in the Greater London conurbation.

Fig. 1.3

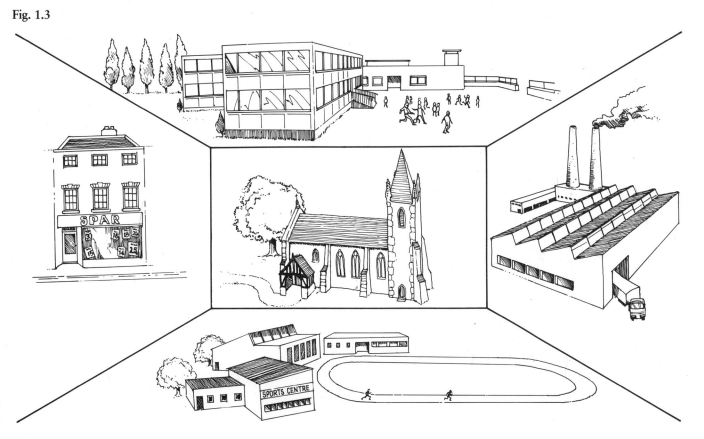

We can also describe how big a settlement is by finding out the amount of land it covers. Use the following method to find out the area of land covered by Bristol and Liverpool.

1 Copy Table 1.2 into your book. Use it to record your results.

Table 1.2

Settlement name	Bristol	Liverpool	
Type	City	City	
1 Number of whole squares covered (1.0)			
2 Number of half squares covered (0.5)			
3 Total number of squares			
4 Area of the settlement (km²)			

2 Start with Bristol (Fig. 1.4). Count up all the whole squares inside the settlement boundary. Enter the number in row 1.

3 Count up all the half squares. Enter this number in row 2. Be careful to remember which squares you have and have not counted. What can you do with the small pieces of square that are left?

4 Add together rows 1 and 2. Put the answer in row 3.

5 In Fig. 1.4 each square covers 4 square kilometres. Multiply row 3 by 4 to find the area of land covered by Bristol. Enter your answer in row 4 of Table 1.2.

6 Work out the area of land covered by Liverpool in the same way.

7 Which city covers most land? How much more land does it cover than the other settlement?

Even though the two settlements are both called cities, they cover a different amount of land. Different towns cover different land areas. The same is true for villages and hamlets.

Work out the area of a classroom (multiply the length of the classroom by its width). If the classroom you choose is not a rectangle discuss a way to work out its area. The things that usually help to make the task easy are:

(i) that, as a rule, we can quickly agree about what is

Fig. 1.4

BRISTOL

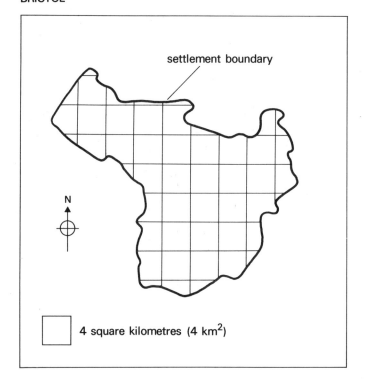

4 square kilometres (4 km²)

LIVERPOOL

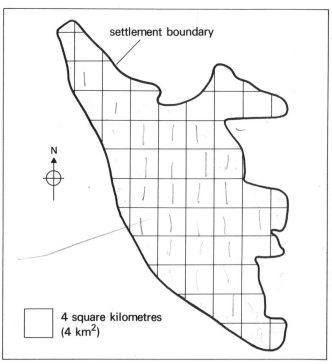

4 square kilometres (4 km²)

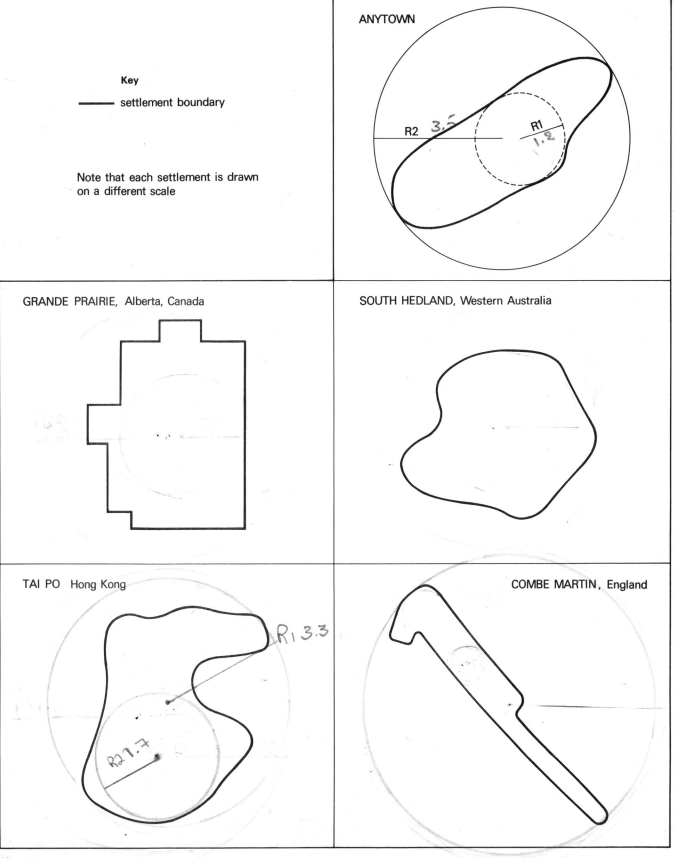

Key

—— settlement boundary

Note that each settlement is drawn
on a different scale

ANYTOWN

R2 3.5   R1 1.2

GRANDE PRAIRIE, Alberta, Canada

SOUTH HEDLAND, Western Australia

TAI PO Hong Kong

R1 3.3

R2 1.7

COMBE MARTIN, England

Fig. 1.5

or is not a classroom. We know what makes it different from the Hall, the Gym and the Staffroom

(ii) that, as a rule, the edge or boundary of the classroom is clear to us. The boundary is formed by the classroom walls. How does the overall size and shape of the room affect this task?

8 Choose one settlement on a map of your local area. Try to work out the amount of land it covers as you did for Bristol and Liverpool. Enter your results in the space left on your table. Make a list of the problems you have in trying to work this out. Try to find out if the settlement is a hamlet, village, town or city. What settlements have others in your class chosen? Does each settlement cover a different area of land? Do you think there is any link between the area and the population of a settlement?

Settlement shape

All the settlements in this book have a different shape. A glance at any map will show you a number of other settlement shapes. One settlement may look round and compact. Another may look spread out. It may look long and thin. This type of settlement is not very compact. The shape of most settlements is difficult to describe as they can have a very irregular shape. Look at the shape of the settlements in Fig. 1.5 (page 5).

1 Write a sentence to describe each settlement shape. (Do not describe the shape of Anytown.)

2 Which settlement looks the most compact?

3 Instead of guessing you can work out your answer in the following way.

(i) Copy Table 1.3 into your book.

(ii) There are four things that you need to do to find out how compact a settlement is.

(a) Using a compass, you need to draw the largest possible circle inside the settlement boundary. This is shown for Anytown in Fig. 1.5

(b) You need to work out the length of the radius of this circle. The radius is a straight line drawn from the centre of the circle to its edge. The length of this radius is called R1 (radius 1). For Anytown R1 is 12 mm. The number is entered in row 1 on the table.

(c) Another circle has to be drawn. This is the smallest possible circle that includes all the settlement. This is again shown for Anytown. The radius of this circle (R2) is then found. It is entered in row 2 on the table.

(d) The shape index tells us how compact a settle-

Table 1.3

Name of settlement	*Example* Anytown	1 Grande Prairie (Alberta)	2 South Hedland (Western Australia)	3 Tai Po (Hong Kong)	4 Combe Martin (S.W. England)
1 Radius of the largest circle drawn inside the settlement (R1)	12 mm				
2 Radius of the smallest circle drawn to include all the settlement (R2)	35 mm				
3 Shape index R1 ÷ R2	0.34				

ment is. To work it out, R1 is divided by R2. The answer is put in row 3. The settlement with a shape index nearest to 1.0 is the most compact settlement. The smaller the shape index, the less compact the settlement.

4 Trace each of the four settlements into your book. With your ruler and compass work out the shape index for each settlement. Enter your results on your table.

5 When you have finished check back to your answer for question 2. Did you guess correctly?

6 Which is the least compact settlement?

7 Write a few sentences to explain why settlements may have different shapes.

Settlement function

If a settlement has a shop people will go there to buy goods. They may buy such things as food, furniture or clothes. The purpose of a shop is to sell things. This is its function. It offers a service to the public. The purpose or function of a factory is to make things. A factory may make things like radios or shoes. The function of a cinema is to entertain people. So different buildings have different functions. Usually, the larger a settlement is, the more functions it has.

1 Look at Fig. 1.6. In each photo a different function is shown. Try to match the photo with one of the functions listed below.

Functions: Manufacturing (making things)   Port
Religious   Tourist   Mining   Capital.

Fig. 1.6

Fig. 1.7

Town or country

Where do you live? Do you live in a city or in a village, town or hamlet? Do you live in a rural (country) area or in an urban (town) area?

1 Look at Fig. 1.7. One photo shows a rural place, the other an urban place. Describe each photo carefully. Be sure to include all the things that make you think that one is a rural and the other an urban place. Consider things like:
  (i) number of buildings
  (ii) use of buildings
  (iii) amount of open space around the buildings
  (iv) use of the open space.

Nearly 76% of the people who live in the United Kingdom live in urban places. This means that 76 out of every 100 people live in towns or cities. Table 1.4 shows how this compares with some other places in the world.

Table 1.4 (based on 1979 World Population Data Sheet)

Place	% living in . . .	
	urban places	rural places
1 United Kingdom	76	24
2 Australia	86	14
3 Singapore	100	0
4 Niger	9	91
5 India	21	79
6 Developing world (the poorer countries)	30	70
7 Developed world (the richer countries)	70	30

2 Copy Fig. 1.8 onto a piece of graph paper. The percentages living in urban and rural places in the United Kingdom have been plotted for you. Use Table 1.4 to plot the other percentages in the same way. Show the urban and rural columns in different colours. Write a few sentences to explain what your graph shows.

Where to build

Settlements begin for many different reasons. Can you give a reason why your settlement started? This is not an easy question. It may depend on your local knowledge. This exercise may help you answer the question.

1 Imagine you are a settler. One day you decide to search for a new place to start a settlement. You take some supplies which provide you with food and water. You also take a tent for shelter at night. As you explore you discover many different landscapes. In some places there are high mountains, in others level plains. There is fresh water in rivers and plenty of vegetation. Some places are sheltered, others open and exposed to the weather. Some places are wet and boggy, others are well-drained. You travel along some river valleys, these are quite easy routeways. Getting over mountains is more difficult.

2 You record what you see by drawing sketches. After two weeks you have drawn five sketches (see Fig. 1.9). On your way back to your old settlement you decide which of the five places is going to provide a site for the settlement you are planning to start. Which place do you choose? Select either (a), (b), (c), (d) or (e). Give reasons for your choice.

3 You hope that the new settlement will grow and not remain isolated. What might attract people to come to the settlement? Think about:
  (i) how easy it is to get to the settlement
  (ii) suitable land for more buildings
  (iii) buying and selling of goods.

Fig. 1.8

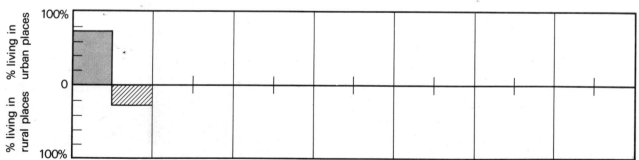

9

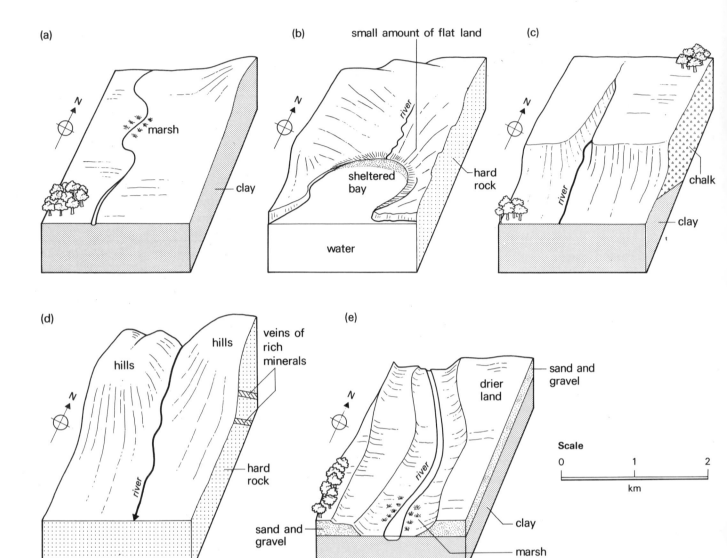

(a)

N

marsh

clay

(b)

small amount of flat land

river

sheltered bay

hard rock

water

(c)

N

river

chalk

clay

(d)

hills

hills

veins of rich minerals

N

river

hard rock

sand and gravel

(e)

N

drier land

river

sand and gravel

marsh

clay

sand and gravel

Scale

0   1   2

km

Fig. 1.9

Fig. 1.10

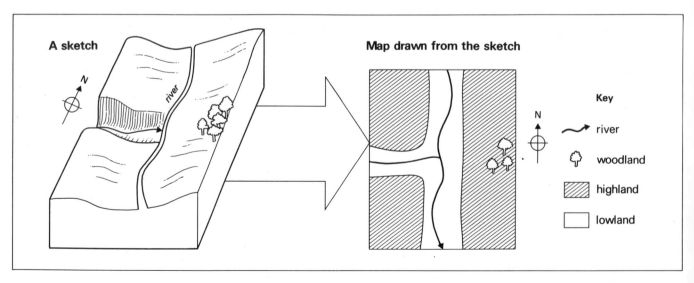

A sketch

N

river

Map drawn from the sketch

Key

N

river

woodland

highland

lowland

4 You also decide to draw a map from your chosen sketch. It will show people where the new settlement is to be. Fig. 1.10 shows you how to draw a map from a sketch. Draw your map in a box 6 cm × 7 cm. Draw on your map the important landmarks. Mark the site for the new settlement with a cross. Think of some ways to show things like:

(i) a river   (ii) trees   (iii) high land
(iv) flat land   (v) marsh.

Giant cities

Giant cities are found all over the world. Table 1.5 is a list of those giant cities which had a population of more than 2 million people in 1980. The latitude (distance north or south of the equator, in degrees) of some of these cities is given.

1 Use the index of an atlas to find the latitude of the others. Record these on a piece of paper.

Table 1.5

City	Area	Latitude	City	Area	Latitude
LONDON	Europe	52N	ATHENS	Europe	
PARIS	Europe	49N	BUDAPEST	Europe	
BERLIN	Europe	53N	KIEV	Europe	
MOSCOW	Europe	56N	SAN FRANCISCO	North America	
LENINGRAD	Europe	60N	WASHINGTON	North America	
MADRID	Europe	40N	PITTSBURGH	North America	
ROME	Europe	42N	ST. LOUIS	North America	
NEW YORK	North America	43N	BALTIMORE	North America	
CHICAGO	North America	42N	CLEVELAND	North America	
LOS ANGELES	North America	34N	HOUSTON	North America	
PHILADELPHIA	North America	40N	CANTON	Eastern Asia	
DETROIT	North America	42N	CHUNGKING	Eastern Asia	
BOSTON	North America	42N	YOKOHAMA	Eastern Asia	
TORONTO	North America	44N	NAGOYA	Eastern Asia	
MONTREAL	North America	46N	SEOUL	Eastern Asia	
TOKYO	Eastern Asia	36N	PUSAN	Eastern Asia	
SHANGHAI	Eastern Asia	31N	TAIPEI	Eastern Asia	
PEKING	Eastern Asia	40N	RANGOON	Southern Asia	
TIENTSIN	Eastern Asia	39N	KARACHI	Southern Asia	
HONG KONG	Eastern Asia	22N	LAHORE	Southern Asia	
OSAKA	Eastern Asia	35N	SINGAPORE	Southern Asia	
SHENYANG	Eastern Asia	42N	BANGKOK	Southern Asia	
WUHAN	Eastern Asia	31N	SAIGON	Southern Asia	
CALCUTTA	Southern Asia	23N	MANILA	Southern Asia	
BOMBAY	Southern Asia	19N	TEHRAN	Southern Asia	
DJAKARTA	Southern Asia	6S	BAGHDAD	Southern Asia	
DELHI	Southern Asia	29N	ISTANBUL	Southern Asia	
MADRAS	Southern Asia	13N	SANTIAGO	Latin America	
RIO DE JANEIRO	Latin America	22S	GUADALAJARA	Latin America	
SÃO PAULO	Latin America	24S	CARACAS	Latin America	
BUENOS AIRES	Latin America	47S	ALEXANDRIA	Africa	
MEXICO CITY	Latin America	19N	KINSHASA	Africa	
LIMA	Latin America	12S	SYDNEY	Oceania	
BOGOTA	Latin America	5N	MELBOURNE	Oceania	
CAIRO	Africa	30N			

2 Copy Table 1.6 into your book. Starting at the top of the list of giant cities, record their location in the world by a tick in the correct box as shown e.g. London 52 degrees north latitude. Count up the number of ticks in each box. Draw a histogram as shown in Fig. 1.11 to illustrate your results.

Table 1.6

	Degree of latitude					
	0–10	11–20	21–30	31–40	41–50	51–60
North of equator	✓					✓✓
South of equator			✓			

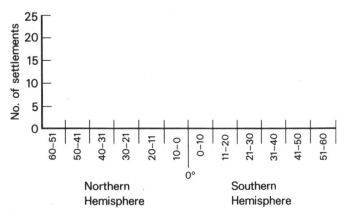

Fig. 1.11

✓ **3** (i) With the help of an atlas, describe where most of the giant cities in the world are found.

(ii) Give two reasons why you think they are found there.

All alone

There are only a few settlements today that are cut off from all others. The ones that are, are usually found in very remote areas. They may be hidden deep in the jungle or in high and mountainous areas. Some settlements are found in places where they become isolated for certain periods of time. For example a scientific research station in Antarctica may exist in isolation for several months. However, between most settlements there is a constant movement of people, goods, money and ideas. Look at Fig. 1.12. It shows two settlements that become isolated for certain periods of time.

Fig. 1.12

1 Describe what it might be like to live in each of these settlements. Think about:

(i) how you could get to the settlement

(ii) what might happen if you became ill

(iii) what you might do in your spare time

(iv) what you might miss most from living in your present settlement

(v) what the advantages might be of living in each of these settlements.

2 Can you think of a reason why each of these settlements started?

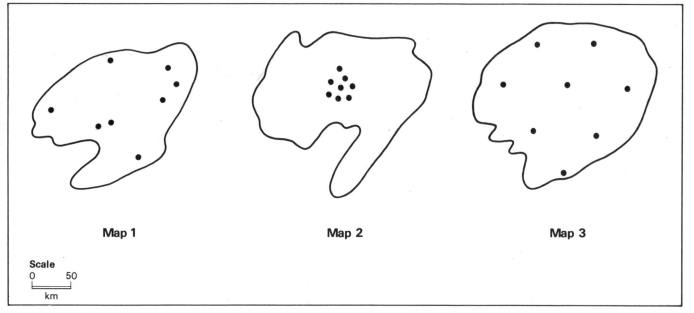

Map 1   Map 2   Map 3

Scale
0   50
km

Fig. 1.13

Fig. 1.14

Settlement pattern

Look at Fig. 1.13. It shows three maps. The dots on each map are settlements with a population greater than 100 000. Although they are shown as dots, they are sprawls of urban land use.

1 On which map are the settlements:
(i) grouped as near as possible to each other. (clustered pattern)
(ii) spread out as far apart as possible from each other.   (uniform pattern)
(iii) neither (i) nor (ii).   (random pattern)

2 Copy each map into your book. Give them their correct pattern names.

3 The pattern of some large settlements in the North Rhine–Westphalia area of West Germany is shown in Fig. 1.14(a).

(i) Do you think the settlements found in this area form a random, clustered or uniform pattern on the ground?

(ii) Find out the special name given to the important industrial area of West Germany inside box A. With this knowledge give one explanation for the settlement pattern in North Rhine–Westphalia.

(iii) Describe the pattern of settlements shown in Fig. 1.14(b). Look at an atlas map of this area. Can you see why line X–Y is important? Give one reason why the largest settlements in Switzerland are north of line X–Y.

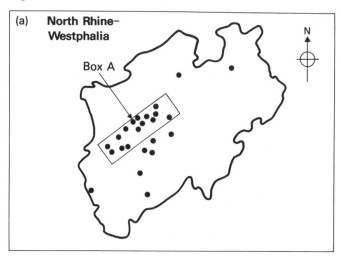

(a) **North Rhine–Westphalia**

Box A

Key
● settlements with a population over 100 000

Scale
0   50
km

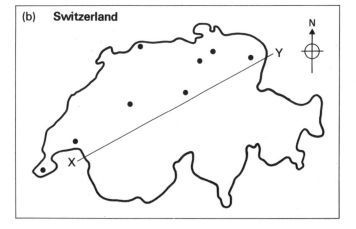

(b) **Switzerland**

Y

X

13

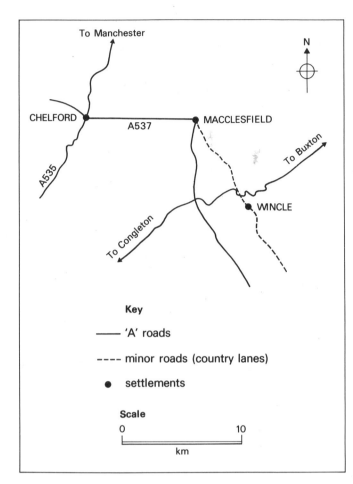

Fig. 1.15 A simplified road map showing some routes between Wincle, Macclesfield and Chelford

Meeting our needs

Many settlements serve the needs of the people in the surrounding area. In order to do this settlements must be accessible. In other words people must be able to travel to them. People and goods must be able to get to the settlements easily.

Look at Fig. 1.15. Imagine that you live in Chelford. You want to do some special shopping. You want to buy a wrist watch, some perfume and a jacket. As you cannot buy these things in your village, you decide to travel to the nearby town of Macclesfield. In this town you have a better range of goods from which to choose. You want some help in choosing your goods. You arrange to meet a friend in the town centre. Your friend lives in Wincle.

1 Is the location of Macclesfield equally handy for both of you? Suggest three things that could affect the ease or difficulty that you and your friend might have in getting to Macclesfield.

Businessland UK

What do you think makes a city important? Do you think it is the number of skilled workers it has? Is it the amount of land it has for future factory and shop development? Some people say that Birmingham is the second most important city in the United Kingdom.

Fig. 1.16 suggests some reasons why Birmingham is such an important city.

1 What is the name of the Metropolitan County in which Birmingham is found?

2 Guess where the centre of the County is. You can locate it more accurately if you first trace around the outline of this Metropolitan County. Now transfer the shape of the County onto a piece of thin card. Cut out its shape. Try to balance the outline on the end of a sharp pencil. Move the card around until the cut-out balances on the pencil. This is the centre of the area. Is Birmingham at the centre point?

3 Fig. 1.16 also shows an advertisement for Birmingham. What is the advertisement suggesting? Is it suggesting that there are some advantages in Birmingham for:
   (i) a shop keeper (retailer)
   (ii) a factory owner (industrialist)
   (iii) a builder (property developer)
   (iv) an hotelier?
Write a few sentences to explain what you think.

4 Every settlement offers something to the people who live there. That is why the settlement is there. Draw an advertisement which advertises what you think your settlement has to offer people. For example if you live in a small hamlet your advertisement may try to suggest openness, greenness and the 'get-away-from-it-all' feeling. When you have finished show your advertisement to someone else in the class. What do they say your advertisement suggests? Do they get the messages you hoped they would? If not, what did your advertisement suggest to them?

5 It would be wrong for us to think that all settlements are in the centre of the area they serve. Where is London? Find it in an atlas. London is the capital of the United Kingdom. As the capital, London serves the whole country. It performs national functions. For example, it is the centre of government. Although London is not centrally located within the UK it still developed as the major city. Try to discover why you think this has happened.

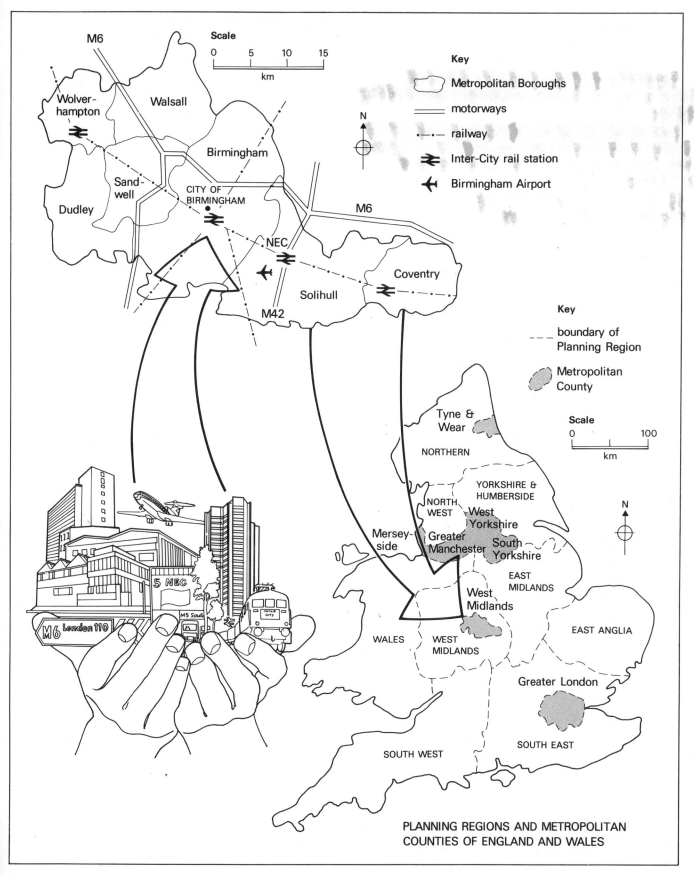

Key

- Metropolitan Boroughs
- motorways
- railway
- Inter-City rail station
- Birmingham Airport

Key

- boundary of Planning Region
- Metropolitan County

M6

Wolver-hampton

Walsall

Birmingham

CITY OF BIRMINGHAM

Sandwell

Dudley

NEC

M6

Coventry

Solihull

M42

Scale

0   5   10   15
km

N

Scale

0   100
km

N

Tyne & Wear

NORTHERN

YORKSHIRE & HUMBERSIDE

NORTH WEST

West Yorkshire

Mersey-side

Greater Manchester

South Yorkshire

EAST MIDLANDS

West Midlands

EAST ANGLIA

WALES

WEST MIDLANDS

Greater London

SOUTH EAST

SOUTH WEST

5 NEC

M6 London 110

M5 South

INTER CITY

PLANNING REGIONS AND METROPOLITAN COUNTIES OF ENGLAND AND WALES

Fig. 1.16

15

Catchment areas

Where people go to shop depends on many things. For example:

(i) the length of the journey. This is the total distance, in kilometres, from home to a shop and back again.

(ii) how easy it is to make the journey. This is affected by the time and cost it takes to make the journey. What other things might affect how easy or difficult a journey is?

(iii) how attractive other shops are.

(iv) the type of goods wanted.

The catchment area is the area from which a city draws its trade. The catchment area contains the catchment population. This is the population which goes to a settlement to buy things. Worcester's shopping catchment area in 1980 is shown in Fig. 1.17(a).

1 The catchment area boundary is shown by the 5% line in Fig. 1.17(a). What is the shape and extent of Worcester's shopping catchment area?

2 What is the link between distance from Worcester and the amount of trade Worcester attracts?

3 Perfectly circular catchment areas are very rare.

Give two examples of landscape features e.g. a line of hills, that might affect the shape of a catchment area.

4 The shape of the catchment area is also affected by other settlements. A person living between two settlements has a choice of shopping place. Look at Fig. 1.17(b). If you lived at:

(i) place A   (ii) place B,

in which of the two settlements are you most likely to go shopping?

If you lived in place C where are you most likely to go shopping? What might influence your choice?

5 Display on the classroom wall a map of your local area. Find your school. Use a pin to mark the place on the map where you live. The others in your class should then do this. Wind some coloured wool around all the points furthest away from your school. What does this line of wool represent? What affects the shape of the catchment area?

6 Choose to study one of the following:

(i) a local dairy   (ii) a bakery   (iii) a newsagents. Find out to where they deliver their goods. Mark these places on a map. Join up the most distant places. Shade in the area inside the catchment boundary. Give your map a suitable title.

Fig. 1.17 (a) Worcester's shopping catchment area (b) Competing shopping catchment areas (based on a City of Worcester Report of Survey)

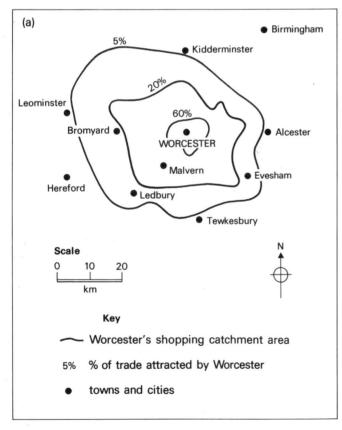

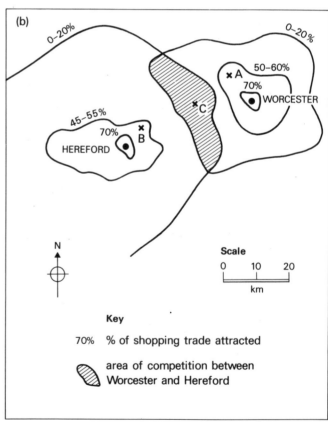

Size and service

Settlements provide services for people who live in and around them. Fig. 1.18(a) shows fifty small settlements in a part of Leicestershire. In this case a small settlement is one which has a population of less than 7500 people. The population of each settlement is given. For example, under 1000 people live in settlement number 50. Fig. 1.18(b) shows the number of services each settlement provides.

Fig. 1.18 (a) Population of selected settlements (b) Number of services for selected settlements (based on Draft Structure Plan for Leicester and Leicestershire)

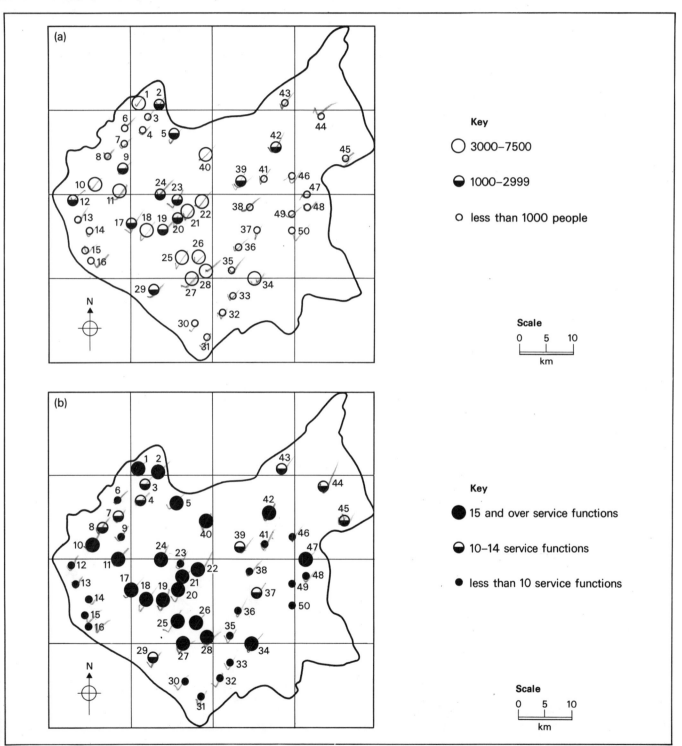

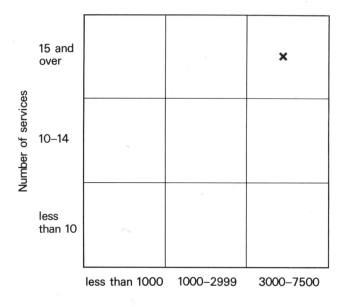

Fig. 1.19

Table 1.7 (based on Leicestershire Draft Structure Plan)

Service	% of settlements in survey with each service
Church	89
Shops	69
Public House	69
Sub Post Office	66
Village/Church Hall	60
Primary School	48
Playgroup	20
Doctor's Surgery	19
Health Centre	16
Further Education Centre	11
Chemist	7
Library	7
Bank	7
Secondary School	4
Police/Fire/Ambulance station	3
Old People's Home	1

1 Copy Fig. 1.19 into your book. Now take each settlement in Fig. 1.18(a) and (b), in turn, and put it in the correct box, by using a cross. Settlement number 1 has been done for you. Notice that it has '15 or more services' and belongs to the '3000–7500' population group. So the settlement is entered in the top right hand corner box.

2 What percentage of the sample has:
(i) a population under 1000 and less than 10 services?
(ii) a population of 3000–7500 and 15 or more services?

3 What do your results tell you about the size of settlements and the number of services they have?

The information in Table 1.7 is for 267 small settlements in Leicestershire. It shows what percentage of this number offer a certain service. For example, 7% of the total number have a library.

4 Which service do most small settlements provide?
5 Why do you think:
(i) a public house   (ii) shops
are found in so many small settlements? What type of shops do you think these would be?
6 Why do you think:
(i) only 4% of the small settlements have a Secondary School?
(ii) only 3% have a Fire/Police/Ambulance station?
7 Think of an interesting way to illustrate all the infomation shown in Table 1.7. Draw the illustration into your book.

City in the rainforest

Sixteen hundred kilometres from the coast of Brazil, along the Amazon River, lies the city of Manaus. Its location is shown in Fig. 1.20. It is the capital of the

Fig. 1.20

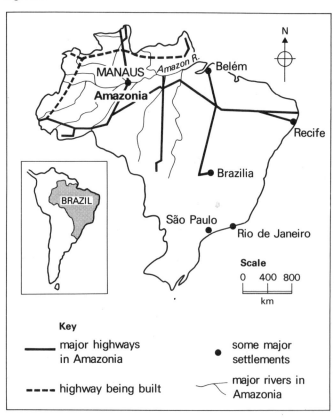

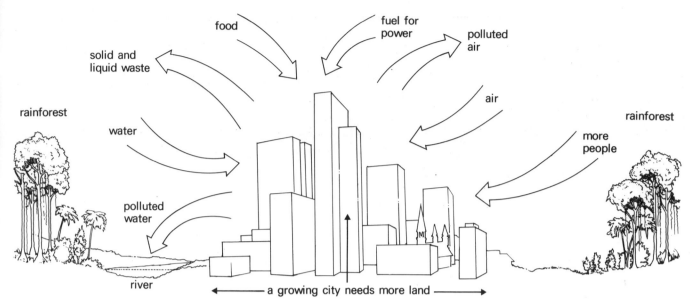

food

fuel for power

polluted air

solid and liquid waste

air

rainforest

water

more people

rainforest

polluted water

river

← a growing city needs more land →

Fig. 1.21 The impact of a growing city on the area around it

state of Amazonia. This is the largest state in Brazil. The city lies deep in the Amazon rainforest.

The rapid growth of Manaus is causing a problem. Some people believe that the growth of this city may cause the death of the plants and animals that live in the forest. In the forest there are about 1000 different types of trees and plants. Fig. 1.21 shows what a growing city, like Manaus, can do to the area around it.

Your class is to have a debate. In the debate you are to discuss this motion: 'that the growth of Manaus should be stopped.'

1 Two groups of speakers should begin the debate. One group should speak for the government of Brazil, who wish to encourage the growth of Manaus. Some others are to represent an Ecology group. This is a group which is keen to stop the forest from being destroyed.

2 Think of some 'other people' who could also speak in the debate. For example:
 (i) a tour operator
 (ii) a Brazilian student studying a rare plant
 (iii) an elderly person who has lived in Manaus all his/her life.

3 You must choose to belong to the Government or Ecology group or decide to be one of the 'other people'. You should aim to write out what you want to say, before the debate begins. Everyone should be prepared to say something. The information given here will help you prepare for the debate. Why not try to find out a little more about life in the Amazon rainforest before the debate begins.

Some Government aims

1 To develop Amazonia carefully and encourage people to go and live there. This means that people will occupy and develop some of Brazil's vast empty spaces.

2 To use the trees and minerals in Amazonia. The Government wants to mine iron ore, tin and bauxite. This will encourage industry to come in to the area. It is already cutting and selling timber but has plans to replant some of the forest land it uses. This is called reafforestation.

3 To encourage the growth of Manaus. Manaus is growing quickly. A few years ago the city could only be reached by air and river. Now it can also be reached by road. The airport has expanded. The boat services have been improved. It has been made a duty free port. This means the making and buying of things is cheaper there than in most places in Amazonia. The population is growing rapidly. In 1969 the population was 180 000. By 1979 it had risen to 500 000. More tourists are also visiting the city and surrounding area.

4 To encourage research into the ways that a city can grow in Amazonia without serious damage to the forest. It has already set up a special settlement called Humboldt City to study this problem.

5 To create forest reserves to protect some of the animals and plants.

Some Ecology Group views

1 The forest should be left alone as it has been for millions of years.

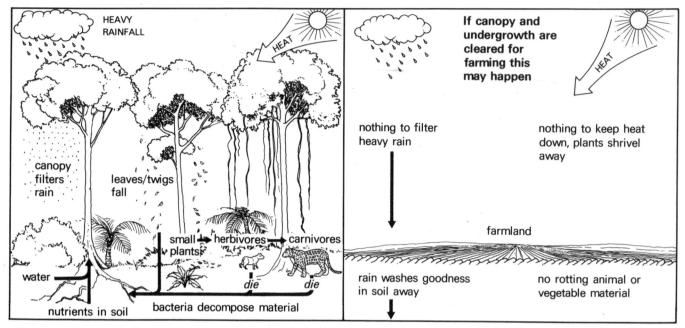

Fig. 1.22 The balance in the rainforest

2 As more land is needed for <u>urban use</u>, the delicate balance of forest life will be upset (see Fig. 1.22).
[handwritten: land use]

3 The Amazon rainforest is one of the world's largest areas of natural beauty. It is an area in which there are:
   200 different kinds of animals
   1500 different kinds of fish
   1800 different kinds of birds.

4 The rainforest provides a large amount of the world's oxygen. Plants take in carbon dioxide and give out oxygen.

Bursting bustee, remedy relocation?

Dacca is the capital of Bangladesh. Find it in your atlas. In 1974 1¾ million people lived in this city. Every year its population grows as more and more people leave the countryside and go to the city. They go to the city searching for work and a better life. Many of the people who arrive in Dacca have little money and no home. As a result they often live in poor and crowded communities called bustees.

In 1974, 170 000 people in Dacca lived in bustee communities. In this year more people than usual arrived in the city. The people who had lost their homes in the floods of that year also flocked into Dacca.

Study Fig. 1.23 carefully. It shows that in 1975 the Bangladesh government moved 70 000 Dacca bustee dwellers into three camps outside the city. It also shows the living conditions in the camps at this time. Using this information:

1 Imagine you are a person who is being moved out of a bustee in Dacca. You are to be resettled in Demra Camp. Describe your feelings the day before you are moved. Contrast this with the way you feel when you see the living conditions in the new camp.

Some people who worked for organisations like Oxfam, visited the three camps in 1975. They wanted to help. They saw that living conditions were rapidly getting worse. They decided that the major problems were:
   (i) lack of food
   (ii) not enough houses
   (iii) no work
   (iv) little sanitation.
Fig. 1.24 shows certain projects started by these organisations to help the people in Demra Camp.

2 How do you think each project has helped to solve the four major problems in Demra Camp? Write a few sentences to explain your answer.

3 Imagine that you have been asked to improve the living conditions in another bustee camp. In what order would you begin the four projects? Give some reasons for your order. The problems are the same as those in Demra Camp. Compare your order with others in your class.

DACCA EARLY 1970s POPULATION 1 730 000

Poor refugees from flooded
areas come to city

Poor people leave the land
looking for WORK in the city

BUSTEES GROW

Poor migrants flock to bustees
There are FEW JOBS – Many have to beg
By 1974 the bustees contained 170 000 people. Massive overcrowding

Government move 40%
to special camps in
1975 (70 000 people)

60% of people
remain in
Dacca's bustees

DEMRA CAMP   TONGI CAMP   BASHAN TEK

At all camps similar conditions
were found:–

                              no money
1   No work

                              lack of
                              food

2   No housing

3   No proper sanitation

4   Poor sites – liable to flood

Fig. 1.23

Fig. 1.24 Four projects started in Demra Camp.
1. Building houses from bamboo. 2. Children learn more modern
ways of growing vegetables. 3. Better sanitation and water supply
4. Women learn domestic skills.

Never the same

Settlements are always changing. They change from hour to hour and day to day. The seasons also bring changes in a settlement.

1 Make a list of the different activities which occur in your settlement:
(i) on a Monday morning between 8.00 a.m. and 9.00 a.m. compared to the activities between 12.00 a.m. and 1.00 p.m.
(ii) on a Saturday morning compared to a Sunday morning.
(iii) in the summer compared to the winter.

2 All sorts of things can change a settlement. Sometimes the changes are very small. Sometimes people's lives are changed completely. What might happen in a settlement if:
(i) all the trains stopped running
(ii) the football team gets to the cup final
(iii) an historic building is demolished to make way for a new office block
(iv) the road which used to run through the settlement is diverted around it?

Over time some settlements grow and prosper while others may prosper and then decay. Settlements can also change their functions. The city of Bristol is shown in Fig. 1.25. Over the years Bristol has grown and prospered. It now has a total population of over 400 000 people. It is the most important commercial and banking centre in South-West England

3 (i) Describe (a) the shape, (b) the amount of land covered by Bristol in 1373.
(ii) Describe how Bristol has changed in its shape and the amount of land it covers (a) from 1373 to 1897, (b) from 1897 to 1980.

From gold town to ghost town

The years 1865–1880 were a period of great gold prospecting in Northern Queensland, Australia. Many

Fig. 1.25 (after Bristol City Planning Department)

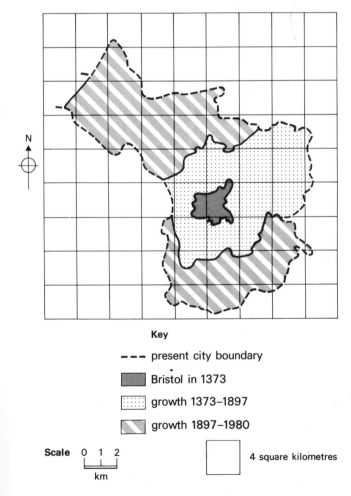

Key
- - - present city boundary

▨ Bristol in 1373

▦ growth 1373–1897

▧ growth 1897–1980

Scale 0 1 2 km

☐ 4 square kilometres

Fig. 1.26 (after G. C. Bolton: *A Thousand Miles Away*)

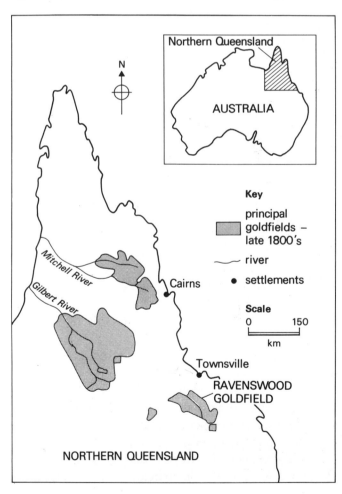

Key

▨ principal goldfields – late 1800's

— river

• settlements

Scale 0 150 km

Fig. 1.27 Ravenswood today

people chased every rumour of gold. In 1868 gold was found at Ravenswood, 88 kilometres south of Townsville. The main goldfields in Northern Queensland at this time are shown in Fig. 1.26 (page 23). Thomas Aitkin, a farmer, discovered the gold at Ravenswood. Word spread quickly about this gold strike and people rushed into the area.

Imagine you visit Ravenswood today (see Fig. 1.27). As you walk along the dusty street past the hotel and general store, you see plenty of things which suggest to you that it was once a booming gold town. You see old mine workings and some old machinery used to crush the rock and separate the gold from other minerals like copper and zinc.

As you wander through the ruins of one building you discover an old grey chest partly hidden under some rocks. You manage to open it. Inside you find lots of papers, a map, a pair of old boots and a note book. You become excited with your discovery. You pick up the note book and find that it belonged to Bill Hodges,

a journalist. Hodges lived in Ravenswood at the time of the gold rush. Inside the note book are a series of labelled sketches. Four of these sketches are shown in Fig. 1.28. The sketches show how Ravenswood grew, prospered but then decayed.

1 Imagine you are the people suggested at the bottom of each sketch, living in Ravenswood in the period shown. Write a paragraph which describes an important day in your life. This will show you the changing fortunes of this settlement during the gold rush period.

2 Find out if there is a place in your own area which has grown, prospered and then decayed. Try to dicover why the place grew and why it decayed. This task invites you to do lots of different things. For example, you may like to talk to your history teacher about it. You might look at books in your school or local library, or at maps, or even perhaps visit the place you are studying.

24

1868 SEARCHING.

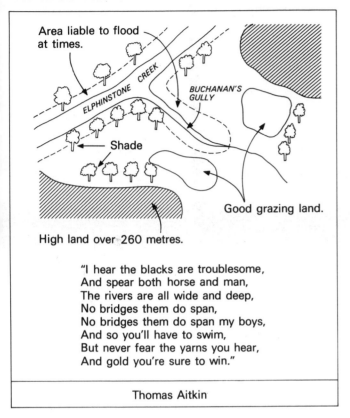

Area liable to flood at times.

ELPHINSTONE CREEK

BUCHANAN'S GULLY

Shade

Good grazing land.

High land over 260 metres.

"I hear the blacks are troublesome,
And spear both horse and man,
The rivers are all wide and deep,
No bridges them do span,
No bridges them do span my boys,
And so you'll have to swim,
But never fear the yarns you hear,
And gold you're sure to win."

Thomas Aitkin

1870 DISCOVERY: TOP CAMP AND EARLY MINES.

Canvas (tent) village. Population 140

Life hard

Flour for cooking scarce.

Little ventilation— temperatures over 38°C.

Piles of gold ore.

Mine entrance.

Gold found in reefs underground.

Many smoked pipes.

Limited water.

Gold ore carried in carts pulled by donkeys/mules.

Liquor plentiful.

One pair of boots for 1 oz. gold.

A mine worker.

1875–1900 BOOM! DEVELOPMENT OF THE TOWN.

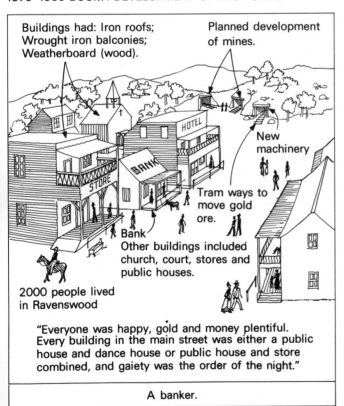

Buildings had: Iron roofs; Wrought iron balconies; Weatherboard (wood).

Planned development of mines.

HOTEL

New machinery

BANK

STORE

Tram ways to move gold ore.

Bank

Other buildings included church, court, stores and public houses.

2000 people lived in Ravenswood

"Everyone was happy, gold and money plentiful. Every building in the main street was either a public house and dance house or public house and store combined, and gaiety was the order of the night."

A banker.

1900–1920 DISAPPOINTMENT AND DECAY.

STORE

Reefs worked out. Reefs too steep.

CLOSED

Ore contained too many impurities.

Lack of geological knowledge.

Mules packed ready to leave. Miners leaving.

A mine worker.

Fig. 1.28 (quotations from G. C. Bolton: *A Thousand Miles Away*)

Hinton becomes a mountain playground

Hinton is a growing town in Alberta, Canada. Today it provides home and work for 7000 people (see Figs. 1.29 and 1.30).

Hinton has grown in an interesting way. Over the period of time shown in Table 1.8, people's work in Hinton has changed.

Study Table 1.8, on page 27, carefully.

Fig. 1.29 Hinton today

Fig. 1.30

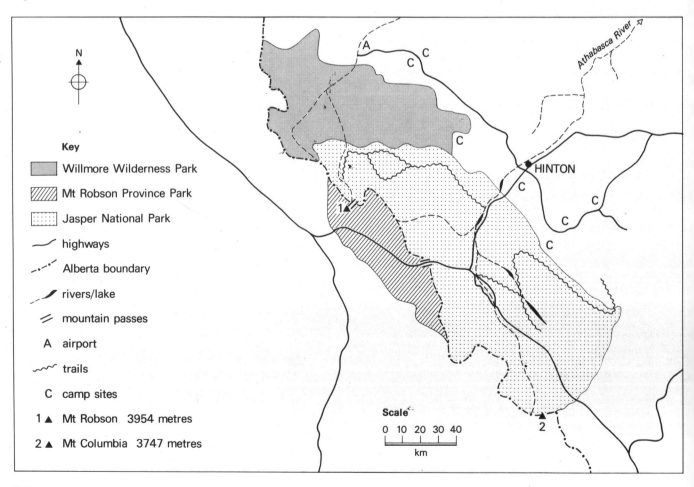

Key

Willmore Wilderness Park

Mt Robson Province Park

Jasper National Park

highways

Alberta boundary

rivers/lake

mountain passes

A airport

trails

C camp sites

1 ▲ Mt Robson 3954 metres

2 ▲ Mt Columbia 3747 metres

Scale

0 10 20 30 40

km

HINTON

Athabasca River

Table 1.8

Period	Reasons for growth	Reasons for decay
1 Before 1900	1 Located on the bank of the Athabasca River. 2 Settlers drawn to the area by the possibility of fur trading and hunting.	1 After a while the settlers moved on. They found it hard to make a living.
2 1908–11	1 Building of the Grand Trunk Pacific Railroad. This linked the Pacific coast settlements with those east of the Rocky Mountains.	1 Lines and trestles laid, the workers and their families moved on.
3 1924–41	1 Large scale coalmines open near to Hinton.	1 Production stops in 1941. The population of Hinton drops to 100.
4 1943–48	1 Local oil exploration and drilling.	1 Limited success. People moved away.
5 1955–70	1 The North West Pulp and Paper Company makes 7800 square kilometres of timber available near Hinton. 2 A 52 million dollar wood pulp plant is built. Wood pulp is used for paper making. 3 Hinton develops to accommodate the mill workers.	
6 After 1970	1 The development of the tourist industry. (a) Hinton becomes a centre for hunting, fishing, camping, mountaineering and trail riding. (b) Hot Springs, Ice Fields and National Parks are within easy reach. (c) Tourism increases the demand for souvenir shops, hotels and motels. Also the building of a cinema and bowling alley, hospital and clinic.	

1 Use the information in Table 1.8 to draw a diagram which shows the different stages in Hinton's development. Try to show that each boom was set off by a different cause. Note also that some boom periods were followed by a short period of decay. Illustrate your diagram by drawing some pictures.

2 Imagine you are a member of the Hinton Chamber of Commerce. In this Chamber of Commerce there are five groups of people. The groups are concerned with:

(a) shop facilities   (b) recreation   (c) transport
(d) accommodation   (e) conservation.

Choose to be a member of one of these groups. This will be your role. The Mayor of Hinton has asked the members of the Chamber to produce a magazine called, 'Hinton: The Gateway to the Rockies'. This magazine should promote Hinton as a centre for tourism.

3 With the others in your group:
(i) make a list of the things you think tourists might need in Hinton. For example the transport group might include some things like (a) twenty-four hour garages (b) easy car hire.

(ii) write some short articles for the magazine. For example the conservation group may want to write articles on topics like (a) camp fires (b) a day in the life of a Forest Ranger.

(iii) design a series of advertisements. For example the accommodation group might design some eye-catching advertisements for a variety of hotels and motels.

4 Think of some other things to be included in the magazine.

2 A look inside settlements

What do you see?

Look out of your classroom window. Do you see buildings and playing fields? Do you see houses and roads? What do you see? What do you see in the area where you live? Do you see the area as a clean and colourful place? Or is it a grim and grubby place? Do you see it as a warm and friendly place? Is it busy and noisy or quiet and rather lonely?

1   Think of some more words. The words must describe what you think of:
   (i) the area where you go to school
   (ii) the area where you live.
Make two lists of words. Compare your list with others in your class. What do you find?

A community is made up of people who live, work and play in one area. People see their community in very different ways. A postman may see his community as a collection of letter boxes. A doctor may see his community as a collection of sick people. Also some things about our community stand out in our minds. For the postman it might be 21 Bridge Street, the house with the angry dog.

2   Look at the list of people below. Do any of them live or work in your community? Write a few sentences to describe how each person might see the place where they live or work:
   (i) an elderly person
   (ii) a two year old child
   (iii) a dentist
   (iv) a librarian.

Fig. 2.1

The use of land

Every settlement has buildings and open spaces. A settlement may have house, shop, factory or farm buildings. It may have a park, pond or gardens. These are types of open space.

1 Look at Fig. 2.1. It shows some of the ways land can be used. You have to decide what the land is being used for and then copy and complete Table 2.1. Note also that you have to put the way land is being used into one of these general groups:

(i) recreation   (ii) industry   (iii) transport
(iv) residential   \ (v) retail.

Table 2.1

Photo	The land is being used for . . .	General land-use group
1		
2		
3		
4		
5		

2 Collect pictures showing different ways land can be used in urban areas. Group together pictures which belong to the same general group. You may need more than five general groups.

Village land use

Look at Fig. 2.2. It shows the types of building and open spaces found in a small Warwickshire village.

1 What are the different types of:
(i) building   (ii) open space
shown on the land-use map of this village?

2 Carefully trace the roads and buildings from Fig. 2.2

3 Colour all the buildings on your map. Show all houses by the same colour. Use another colour for all the public buildings, and so on. Draw a key to go with your map. The key is to show which colours you have used for the different types of buildings.

4 Label your land-use map. Label the areas:
(i) pasture land
(ii) arable land
(iii) old orchard.
Label the roads leading out of the village.

5 Draw a histogram (bar graph) to show how many buildings, of each type, are found in this village. Draw a graph as shown in Fig. 2.3. What does your graph show?

6 Try to visit a small village in your local area. You might discover some more ways village land is used. In what other ways is your village different from the one given here? Try to explain why this is so.

Fig. 2.2 Grandborough village

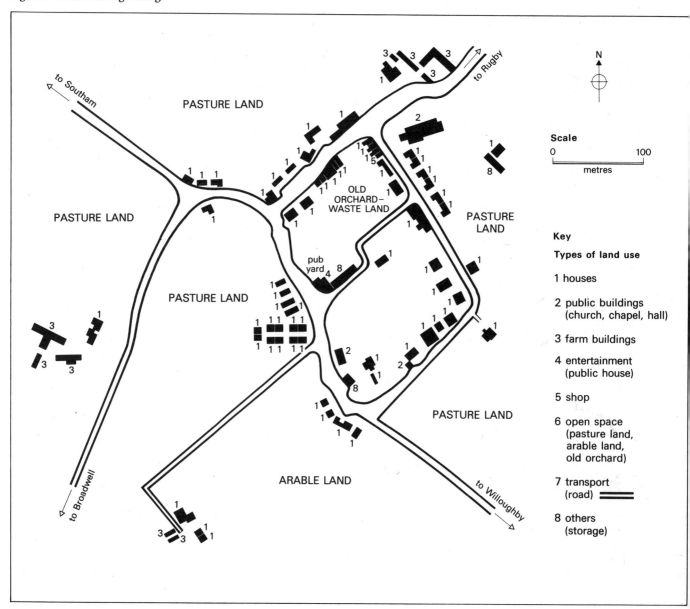

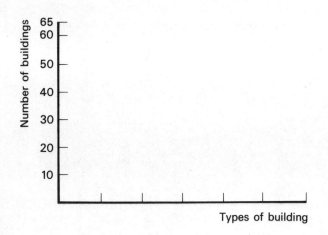

Fig. 2.3

City land use

Another land-use map is shown in Fig 2.4 (page 32). It shows the way the land is used in the City of Worcester.

1 Thinking about:
(i) land use
(ii) amount of land covered,
give four ways that the settlement in Fig. 2.4 is different from that in Fig. 2.2.

2 What is most of the city land used for in Fig. 2.4? It is easy for us to guess this and get the right answer. But sometimes we may need to answer a question such as, 'how much more land is used for housing than for main shopping in the city'? To do this we can use the method described below. It is an alternative to guessing the right answer.

3 Copy Table 2.2 into your book. Use it to record your results.

Table 2.2

Point	Land used for . . .
1	
2	
and so on to . . .	
42	

(i) Place some tracing paper over Fig. 2.4. Trace round the map frame. Divide your tracing paper into 2.5 cm squares, using the marks on the map frame.
(ii) Begin in the north-western (top left hand) corner of the map. This is square number one. Find the centre of this square. Can you suggest ways that you could do this? Use the most accurate of the two ways. The centre of square one is called point one. Does point one fall inside the city boundary? If YES, on what land-use group does it fall? Enter this on Table 2.2. If NO, leave the 'land used for' part of the table blank for this point.
(iii) Move along each row in turn. Find the centre point of every square on your tracing paper. Enter on Table 2.2 the land use of centre points only when they are inside the city boundary.
(iv) Copy Table 2.3 into your book. Using Table 2.2, count up the number of times each centre point has fallen on the same type of land use. Enter these totals on Table 2.3.

Table 2.3

Land-use type	Total number of points for that one land-use type

(v) Use the following to work out how much of the city land is taken up by each type of land use:

$$\frac{\text{total number of points for one land-use type}}{\text{total number of points falling inside the city boundary}} \times \frac{100}{1}$$

= % of total city land used in this way.

For example:
Say we have a total number of 18 points for housing land use . . .

$$\frac{18}{30} \times \frac{100}{1}$$

$$= \frac{3}{5} \times \frac{100}{1}$$

$$= \frac{300}{5}$$

= 60% of the total city land is used for housing.

(vi) Use your answer for 3(v) when answering question 2.

4 Although this method appears to give us an 'accurate' answer, can you see why we should be careful when using it?

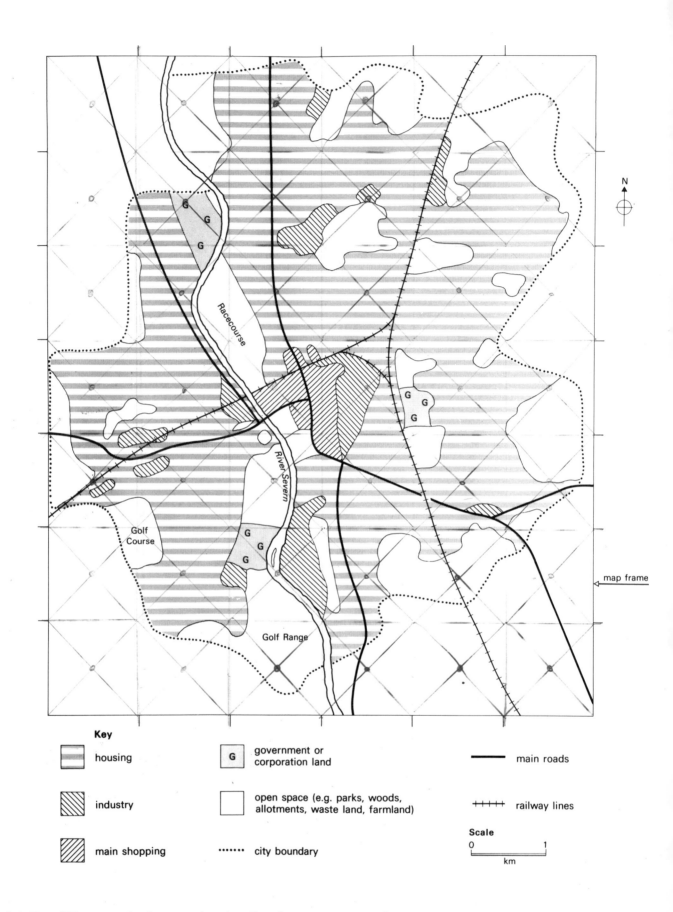

Key

housing		government or corporation land		main roads
industry		open space (e.g. parks, woods, allotments, waste land, farmland)		railway lines
main shopping		city boundary		

G government or corporation land

Scale

0   1
km

Fig. 2.4 City of Worcester – land-use map (based on City of Worcester: Report of Survey, 1972)

Groups inside settlements

Settlements are full of groups: groups of homes, shops, factories and people. In some settlements people and homes are grouped together into communities. These communities can be of different sizes. Some can be quite small and made up of a few buildings and people. They are often called dwelling groups. Neighbourhoods are much bigger types of community. They are made up of many dwelling groups.

Look at Fig. 2.5. It shows a series of communities of different sizes. The smallest community that is shown is called a family unit and is made up of one house and family. The biggest in this series is called a neighbourhood.

1 Draw the diagrams from Fig. 2.5 into your book in the correct order. Start with the smallest community and finish with the biggest. Give each diagram its correct label from this list:

    a family unit (4 people)
    a neighbourhood (up to 8000 people)
    a local cluster (up to 1000 people)
    a dwelling group (about 100 people).

Fig. 2.5 (**after** *Telford Development Proposals, Vol. 1*)

Shopping centres

In any large town or city the greatest number and variety of shops occur in the central area. In the city centre we can usually find shops which sell goods that people need daily and weekly. For example, goods like food, newspapers, sweets and tobacco. These goods are called convenience goods. We can also find shops which sell goods that people tend to buy less often. These goods usually cost a lot of money and are not used-up and finished with quickly. Such goods are furniture, carpets and electrical appliances. These are called durable goods. The shops in a city centre serve a large area and meet the needs of many people.

In most towns and cities goods are also sold in places which lie outside the central area. A big city may even have a limited number of quite large 'district' shopping centres. Most towns and cities have lots of 'local' shops. Local shops serve the needs of local people who live close to them.

Look at Fig. 2.6 overleaf. The photographs show four types of shopping centre.

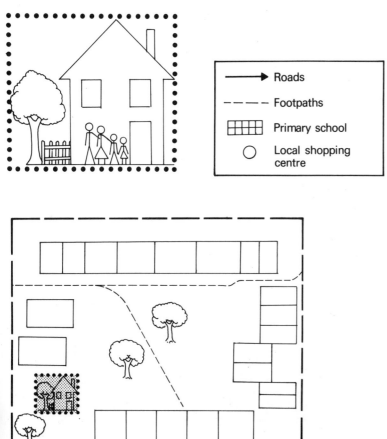

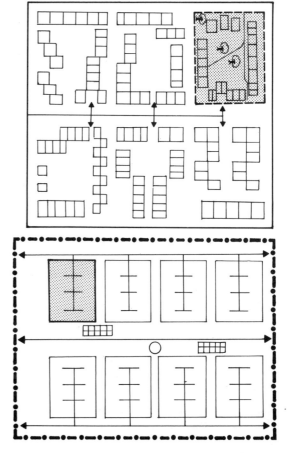

33

Fig. 2.6 Shopping centres

Type of shopping centre

4 Corner shop
2 District shopping centre
3 Local shopping centre
1 City Centre shopping complex

Description of shopping centre

3 May include a small supermarket, newsagent and grocers shop. Half of all visits are daily. 90% of shoppers reach shops by walking. About half an hour spent shopping by most people.

4 Serves a few hundred people. Visits made daily. People usually walk there. They spend up to 10 minutes shopping and do not spend much money.

1 Has a variety of convenience and durable goods shops. Visits mainly weekly or fortnightly, some monthly visits. Many people come to shops by car or bus.

2 Usually have a variety of mainly convenience goods shops. Visits often made weekly. Up to 30% of the people come by car. People spend up to 1 hour shopping.

1) range of goods
2) differ in size
3) number of customers

34

1 In what three ways are the shopping centres different from each other?

2 Copy Table 2.4 into your book.

Table 2.4

Photo	Type of shopping centre	Description of shopping centre
1		
2		
3		
4		

Use the information in Fig. 2.6 to complete Table 2.4. Match the type and description of the shopping centre with the correct photo.

3 Try to visit a place where there is a small, but interesting, group of shops. It may be a shopping precinct, a market square or a small old street of shops. Copy Table 2.5 and use it to record the number of types of shop that you find there.

Table 2.5

Shop type	Number of shops
Group A shops selling mainly convenience goods e.g. grocers, butcher, bakers, off-licence, newsagent	
Group B shops selling mainly durable goods e.g. furniture, hardware, electrical, ironmongery	
Group C others	

(i) Do all your shops fit neatly into Group A or Group B? If not, list those shops that you think do not belong in Groups A or B in Group C.

(ii) Write a few sentences to describe what your results show. Say something about (a) the size of the shopping centre (b) the variety of goods found there. Do your results tell you anything about (a) where the customers might come from? (b) how often people might visit this shopping centre?

Telford's traffic

Figures 2.2 and 2.4 show that roads link one part of a settlement with another. They show that the pattern of roads and the size of roads can affect the shape of a settlement.

For heavy traffic very large roads need to be built. These roads are wide and may even have two carriageways. In Telford New Town these big roads are called primary roads. In Telford some much smaller roads have also been built. These roads carry only a little traffic. They go to people's homes.

Look at Fig. 2.7. It shows a simplified pattern of roads in Telford. On each road there is a number. This tells you how many thousands of vehicles use that road every day.

1 Trace the diagram into your book. Do not trace the numbers, just the lines and dots.

2 Use the numbers and scale given to draw lines of different widths on your diagram. The wider the line, the more traffic flows on that road.

3 The diagram has been started for you. Look carefully at the way you have to join the different width lines together.

4 Study the information in Table 2.6.

Table 2.6 (based on *Telford Development Proposal, Vol. 1*)

Type of road	Number of vehicles using the road each day
1 Primary	over 25 000
2 District	10 000–24 999
3 Local	1000–9999
4 Access	under 1000
(Access roads are not shown on Fig. 2.7).	

On your finished diagram label one: primary road,
district road
local road.

5 Draw a small sketch map to show the pattern made by the primary roads in Telford.

6 If possible try to carry out a traffic flow survey for some of the roads near to your school. If you do this you will need to decide:

(i) which roads are to be surveyed

(ii) where you must stand

(iii) which type of vehicles you must count

(iv) how long you must count vehicles for

(v) how to record your results.

When you return to school you will need:

(i) to find out from others in your class how many vehicles they counted at their own survey point

(ii) a base map which shows all the roads in the survey

(iii) to decide what scale to use to draw different width lines onto your base map as you did for Telford

(iv) to describe what your diagram shows. For example does it show any places where traffic bottlenecks might occur?

7 How might:
 (i) the time of day
 (ii) the length of vehicle counting time
affect the pattern of vehicle movement shown on your traffic flow diagram?

Fig. 2.7 Estimated traffic flow over a 24-hour period in Telford (in thousands of vehicles) (after *Telford Development Proposal Vol. 1*)

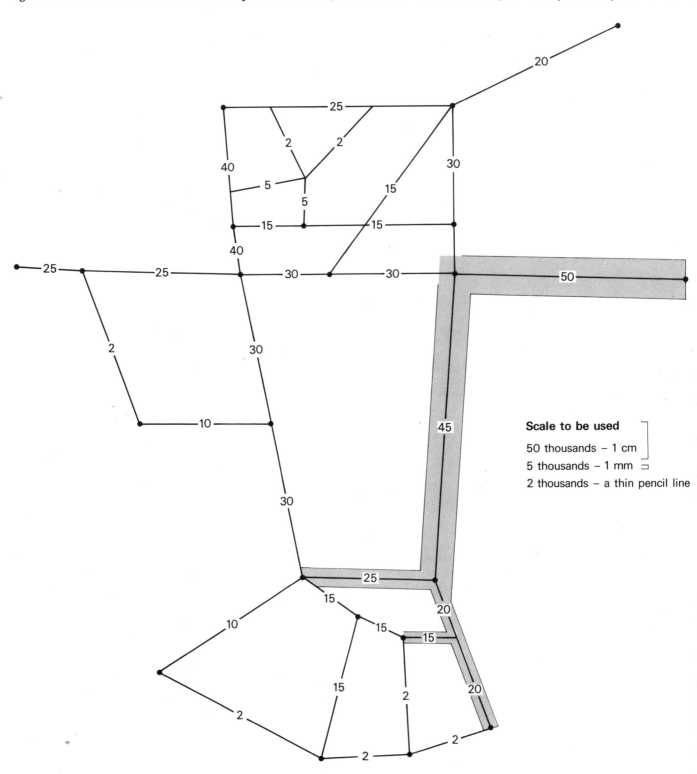

Where is the town centre?

We know from our work on the exercise called 'What do you see' that people see the place where they live and work in different ways. We also know that there are at least two reasons for this. For example it may have something to do with a person's age and the work that they do. The size of a settlement also affects how we see it. It affects our knowledge of it. In a small village we may quickly agree where 'the Green' or the Church is. In larger settlements these terms may mean a different place to different people. Why do you think this is so?

1 Think about the settlement where you live. Where do you think the centre of your settlement is? Describe its location in words. Try also to pin-point it on your local map. Do others in your class agree with you?

Fig. 2.8 is a map of part of the settlement of Stratford-upon-Avon. Stratford gets a lot of overseas tourists. Many American, Japanese and European people go

Fig. 2.8 A tourist view of Stratford-upon-Avon's town centre

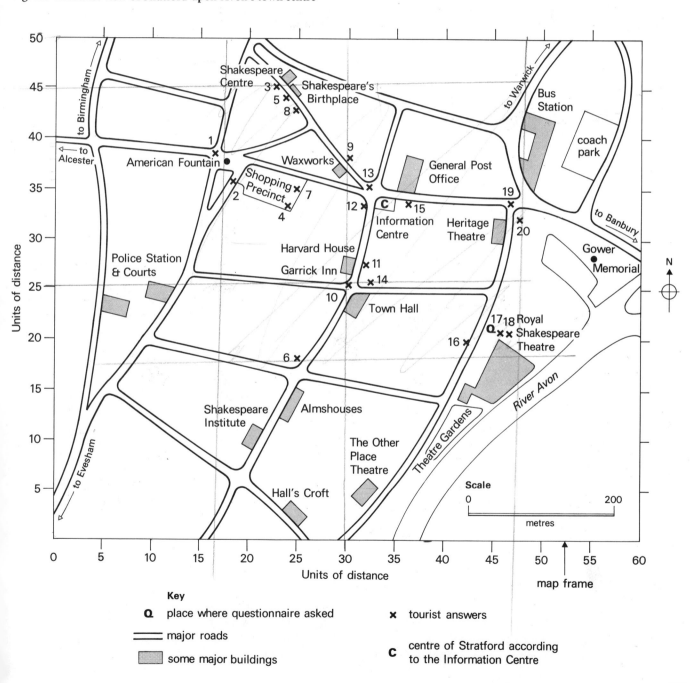

Key

Q place where questionnaire asked

major roads

some major buildings

✗ tourist answers

C centre of Stratford according to the Information Centre

there every year. Twenty overseas tourists were shown a map and asked, 'where do you think the town centre of Stratford is?' The person who asked this question was standing at point Q on the map. The tourist answers are shown by crosses on Fig. 2.8.

2 Why do you think people give lots of different answers? *where do you think the centre is*

This small survey should leave you wondering just where the town centre of Stratford really is! The following method helps us combine the twenty different tourist replies into one answer.

3 (i) Lay some tracing paper over the map of Stratford.

(ii) Join up the marks shown on the map frame to make a squared pattern.

(iii) Label the line along the bottom axis x, and the line up the side axis y. Number each axis as shown on Fig. 2.8.

(iv) Mark carefully on your tracing paper the twenty crosses shown on the base map.

4 Draw Table 2.7 into your book.

Table 2.7

Part	x-axis		y-axis	
	Cross no.	Units of distance	Cross no.	Units of distance
One	1 2 3 4 and so on to . . . 20	17 18 23 24	1 2 3 4 and so on to . . . 20	38 36 45 31
Two	Total of x-axis values =		Total of y-axis values =	
Three	Divide your part two answer by 20 (the number of people asked) This =		Divide your part two answer by 20 This =	

5 Work out part one. Work from left to right along the x-axis. Record the units of distance for each cross on Table 2.7. The first three values from the x-axis and the y-axis have been done for you.

6 Work out parts two and three. At the end of part three you will have two values. One value for each of your two axes. These values are co-ordinates. Plot the co-ordinates on your tracing paper. Where do they

join? Mark the spot with a coloured star. This is the centre of the spread of crosses shown on the map. According to this group of tourists, where is the town centre of Stratford?

7 The people who work in the information centre in Stratford regard place C (shown on the map) as the real town centre. Is it different from where the group of tourists think the town centre is? If yes, explain why this difference occurs.

8 Use this method again to try to pin-point the centre of the settlement where you live. Instead of asking tourists you could ask friends or parents.

Here is a town centre

A town centre is the focus of the whole town. It is a place where many roads come together. Normally it can be easily reached by everyone in the surrounding area. We know that there can be many shops in a town centre. The town centre of Basildon, for example, has over 200 shops. Some of the large 'chain stores' are found there, for example, Marks and Spencer, Sainsbury's, Boots and Littlewoods.

But there are also many other things to be found in a town centre. For example there may be offices, places of entertainment and places to eat.

1 Study Figs 2.9 and 2.10. They show a map and a photo of Basildon town centre. Place a piece of tracing paper over the photo. Using the map and photo together:

(i) mark on and label (a) the Ring Road made up by Broadmayne and Southernhay (b) Roundacre Roundabout (c) the railway line and station

(ii) locate these buildings and number them, on your tracing, using the key

1 = Bowling Alley   2 = Market   3 = Council Offices
4 = Cinema   5 = Bus Terminal   6 = Police Station
7 = St. Martin's Church

Also copy this key into your book.

2 What conclusions can you make about the functions of the buildings found in this town centre? Think of examples of similar 'town centre functions' in a place near to your home or school.

3 In what ways does the map suggest that Basildon town centre can be easily reached by everyone?

4 If you were shopping in the Town Square would you have to worry about danger from vehicles? Explain your answer.

5 Which way was the camera pointing when the photo was taken?

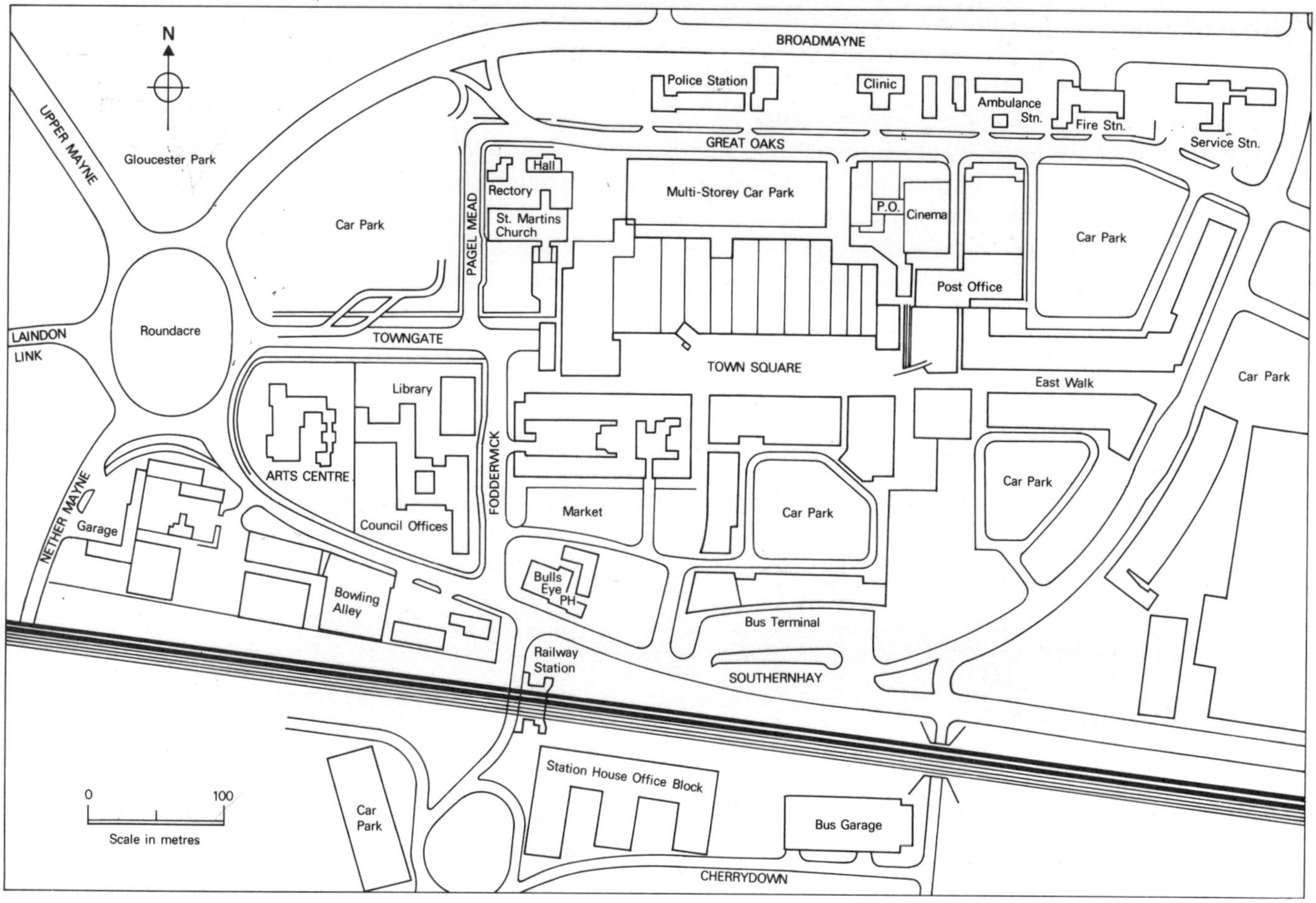
N
BROADMAYNE
UPPER MAYNE
Gloucester Park
Police Station
Clinic
Ambulance Stn.
Fire Stn.
Service Stn.
GREAT OAKS
Hall
Rectory
St. Martins Church
PAGEL MEAD
Multi-Storey Car Park
P.O.
Cinema
Car Park
Car Park
Roundacre
Post Office
LAINDON LINK
TOWNGATE
TOWN SQUARE
East Walk
Car Park
Library
ARTS CENTRE
FODDERWICK
Car Park
NETHER MAYNE
Garage
Market
Car Park
Council Offices
Bulls Eye PH
Bowling Alley
Bus Terminal
Railway Station
SOUTHERNHAY
Station House Office Block
0
100
Scale in metres
Car Park
Bus Garage
CHERRYDOWN

Fig. 2.9 Basildon Town Centre

Fig. 2.10 General view of Basildon Town Centre

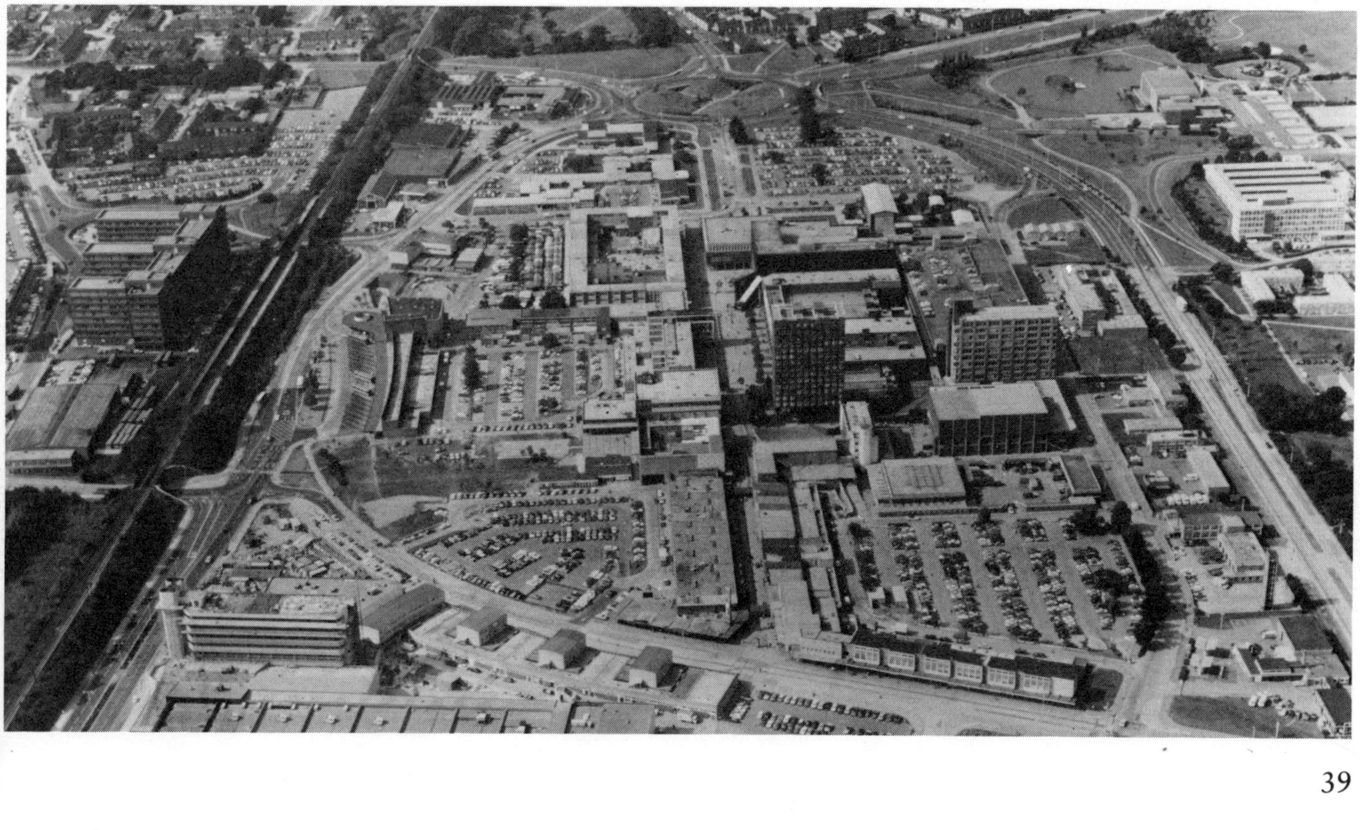

Where do things belong?

The imaginary settlement of Belville is shown in Fig 2.11(a). In Belville there are many buildings and facilities that might be found in any large settlement. For example there are areas of industry, shops, houses and transport facilities. Do you notice anything strange about the location of these things in this settlement? Do you think that some of them just do not belong together? For example the rifle range next to the Infants school!

1 Make a list of examples of things that you think do not belong together. Say why you think they should not go together.

2 Using a tracing of Fig. 2.11(b) place the buildings and facilities shown in Fig. 2.11(a) where you think

Fig. 2.11 Belville

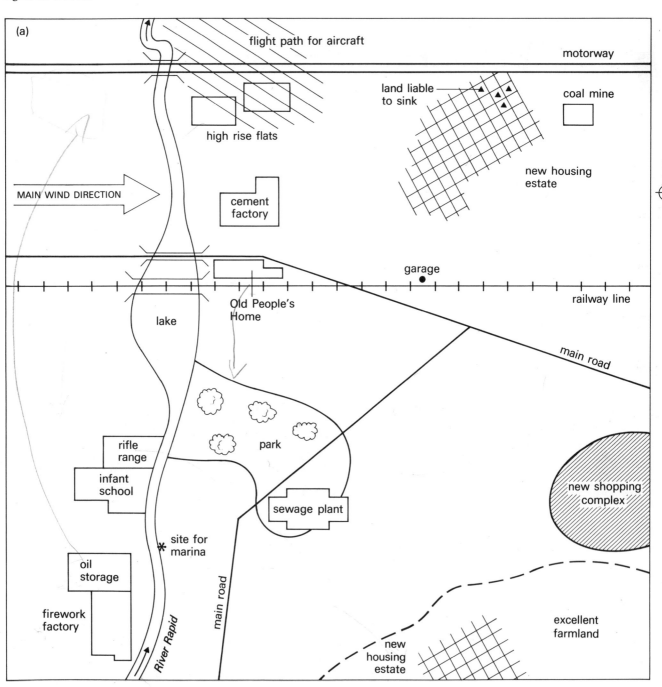

Buildings not drawn to scale

they should belong. For example, take the garage away from the railway line and replace it on a road.

Some functions are best in central locations. They need to be as close as possible to everyone in the area. By being in the centre everyone can get to them easily.

3 Some functions prefer to be near to certain other functions. Look at Fig. 2.12. What examples of this statement do you see in the photos? Explain why you think these functions like to be near to each other.

4 Make a list of the other functions that you think generally like to be near to each other in a town centre. For example do you think restaurants are often near to theatres? Give a reason for each example you think of. A visit to a town centre near to your home or school may help you answer this question.

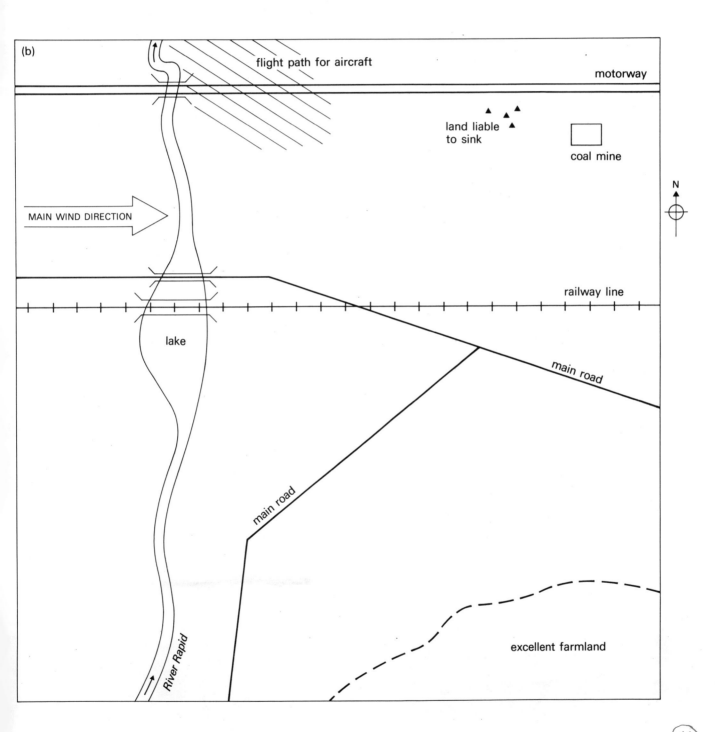

Fig. 2.12

3

4

Within easy reach

Factories are often clustered together in one part of a town. Sometimes these sites are located on the edge of a town. On the edge there is plenty of land for future factory growth. In some settlements industry and homes are kept apart. But people are needed to work in factories and people like to be able to get to work easily. Houses and factories are linked together by roads.

1 Look at Fig. 2.13.
(i) Where are the industrial areas located?
(ii) Give three reasons why you think they are found there.
(iii) Where are the houses located?

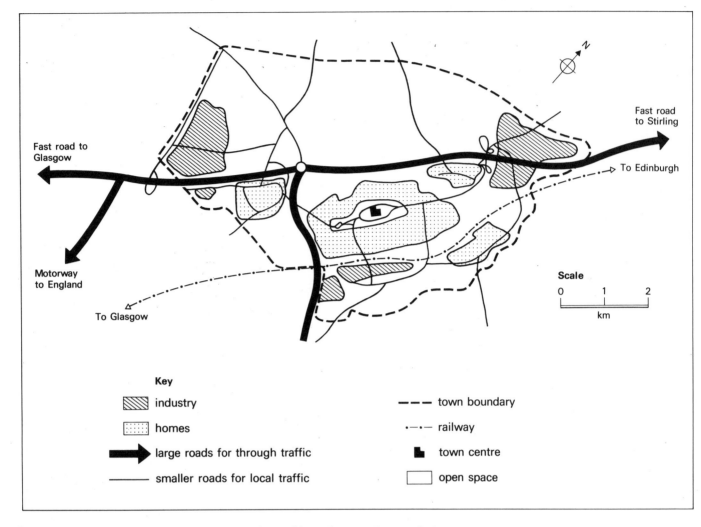

Key

▨ industry	--- town boundary
▨ homes	·—·— railway
➤ large roads for through traffic	■ town centre
— smaller roads for local traffic	▢ open space

Fig. 2.13 Cumbernauld New Town (after Cumbernauld Development Corporation)

(iv) Give two reasons why you think they are found there.

(v) Local traffic is kept apart from through traffic: (a) how is this done? (b) why is this done?

(vi) Why do you think the town centre is located where it is?

Where people live

Have you ever moved from one house to another? When people look for a new place to live they have to make many decisions. Some people may decide to live near to open country or in a house with a garden. Others may decide to live in a flat. Some may choose to be close to their place of work. Some may choose to live near to people they like in some way. Some may have very little choice at all. Look at the four photos in Fig. 2.14. Each photo shows a different area in or near to Greater London.

1 Copy Table 2.8 into your book. Take each photo in turn and make a list of the things you see in each zone. For example things like back-to-back houses, allotments and empty buildings. Write these things in the space left in the table. Do you think any of them are important to people when they are deciding where to live? Explain your answer.

Table 2.8

Area where photo taken	Urban zone	Photo	Things I see in the photo
The City	Inner	A	
Lambeth	Middle	B	
Bexley Heath	Outer	C	
Amersham	Fringe	D	

44

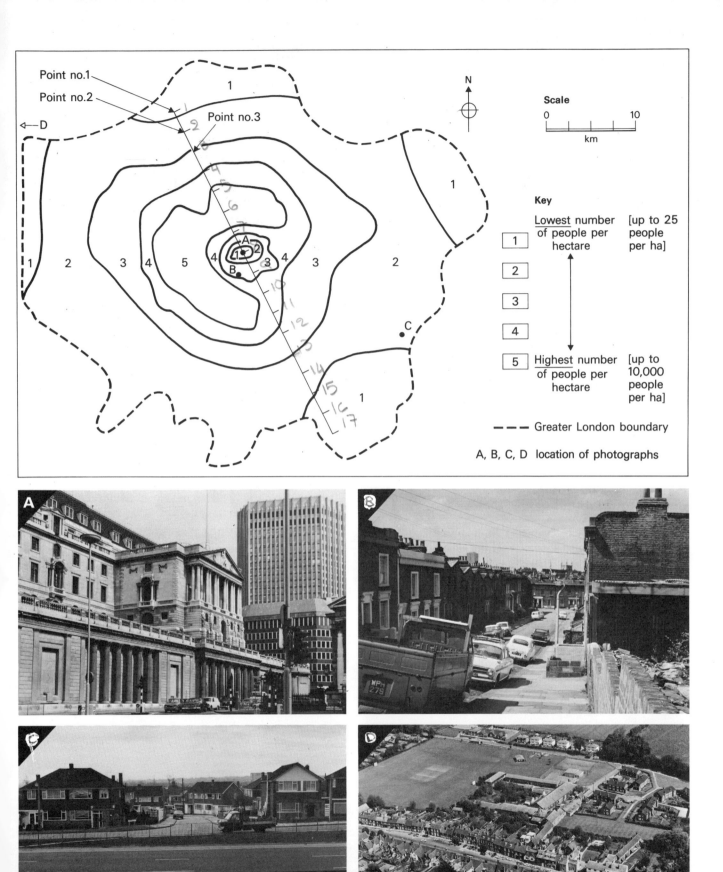

Point no.1
Point no.2
Point no.3

← D

N

Scale
0   10
km

Key

1	Lowest number of people per hectare
2	
3	
4	
5	Highest number of people per hectare

[up to 25 people per ha]

[up to 10,000 people per ha]

- - - Greater London boundary

A, B, C, D location of photographs

A
B
C

Fig. 2.14 A population density map of Greater London (based on *Data in Geography: Cities*, Longman)

Look at the map in Fig. 2.14. It shows the average number of people living on every hectare of land in each part of the Greater London conurbation. This is called its population density. In order to be able to make some sense of this map we first need to be able to describe the population pattern. One way to do this is to draw a cross-section using the line that has been drawn across the map.

2 Draw and label two axes on a piece of graph paper as shown in Fig. 2.15. Find point one on the line on Fig. 2.14. Point one falls in the population density area number one. It has been plotted on the cross-section for you. Move down the line to point number two. Notice that this falls in the population density area number two. This means that more people live in each hectare of land in this area, than in area number one. It has also been plotted on the cross-section along with point three. Continue to move down the line of points. Plot the value of each point on the cross-section. Join up the points in a free hand way to form a curved line.

3 Describe and explain the population density pattern shown by your cross-section, as distance increases from the city centre.

Competition for land

Things that are in short supply have a high value. Accessible places inside settlements are in short supply. These places have a high value. The people who want to have a shop, office, factory or home in a very accessible place have to pay a high price to be there.

They also have to compete with each other for these scarce places. This competition pushes up the price of the land. The land is sold or rented, in most cases, to those who pay the highest prices. So the high cost of land tends to attract only those urban functions which can afford to be there.

Look at Fig. 2.16
1 Make a tracing of the Bristol land-use map. Stick it firmly into your book. Select four colours. Colour your tracing to show clearly the four major types of land use in Bristol. Draw a land-use key separately in your book.

2 Trace the Bristol land-value map. Lay this piece of tracing paper over your land-use map. Stick one edge of the tracing to your book. Draw the land value key separately in your book.

3 What do the two maps together suggest is the link between:
(i) the location of shops and offices and the price of land
(ii) the location of industry and the price of land. Try to explain why each is linked in that way.

4 Write down two examples of the sorts of industry which might:
(i) prefer central accessible locations
(ii) prefer to be located on lower cost land away from the city centre.

5 Why do you think that most houses are not built on the most expensive urban land?

6 Suggest some other things besides competition that might affect the price of land in an urban area. Explain each suggestion.

Fig. 2.15 A cross-section of population density in Greater London

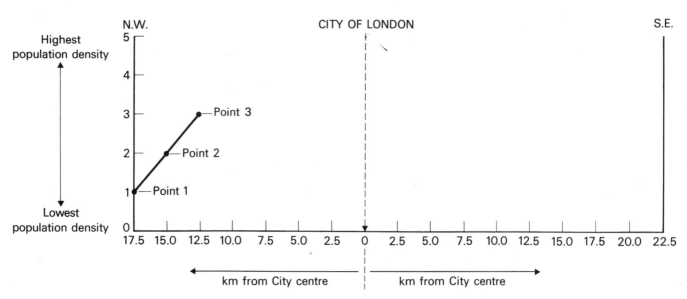

46

Fig. 2.16 (a) **Land use in Bristol** (b) **land value in Bristol** (based on *Data in Geography: Cities*, Longman)

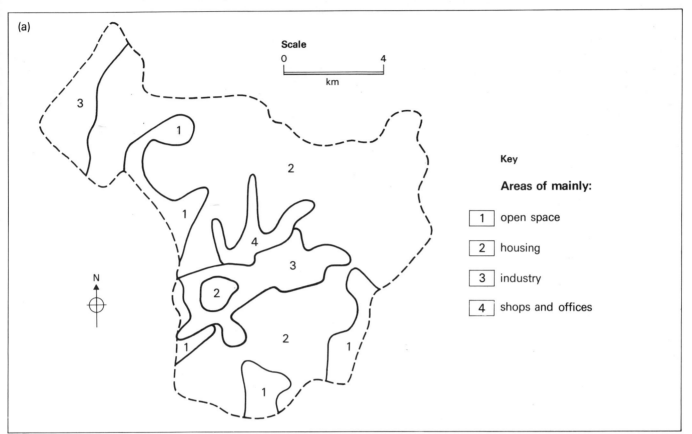

(a)

Scale

Key

Areas of mainly:

1 open space

2 housing

3 industry

4 shops and offices

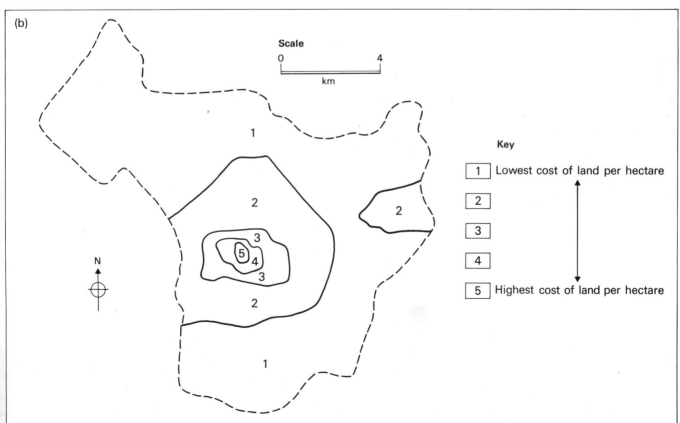

(b)

Scale

Key

1 Lowest cost of land per hectare

2

3

4

5 Highest cost of land per hectare

Who cares?

Inside every settlement in the world there are differences. For example there are differences in the quality of housing and in the amount of open space. The people who live in settlements are also different. They are different in the amount of money they earn and in the quality of their health. There are differences in language, religion, dress, music, food and the place where people were born. All these things make up culture. People who have some of these things in common belong to the same culture group. Look at Fig. 2.17. It shows a number of culture groups which can be found in New York city.

1 The names of the culture groups are:
Negroes, Chinese, Jews and Italians.
Match the photos with the culture groups.

In some parts of New York there are groups of people as shown in Fig. 2.17 who have certain cultural things in common. These things make them different from other inhabitants in the city. The areas where distinct cultural groups live are called ghettos. Ghetto life can have some advantages.

2 How would you support the statement that 'there is a lot to be said for living near to those people who share your own language, customs and beliefs'?

Fig. 2.17

Fig. 2.18

Sometimes when the word ghetto is used people think of human misery and despair. Look at Fig. 2.18. It shows one ghetto in New York city.

3 Make a list of the sorts of problems you think the people who live in the ghetto might have.

Look carefully at Fig. 2.19. It shows a 'poverty trap' that some ghetto dwellers find themselves in. But people can also be caught in a poverty trap without living in a ghetto.

4 Why do you think it is called a poverty trap?
5 What can be done to help ghetto dwellers who are caught in a poverty trap? Imagine you are a ghetto dweller living in an area like the one shown in Fig. 2.18. You have been offered:
   (i) a chance to move out of the ghetto into another part of New York
OR
   (ii) a regular supply of food and medicine.
Which offer would you accept, or would you reject both of them? Explain your answer.

The Poverty Trap

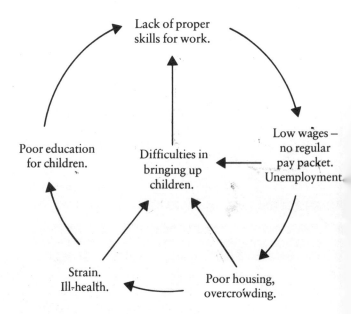

Fig. 2.19

50

Fig. 2.20 Belize

Belmopan: a better city?

Many cities in the world have grown without a plan. Usually city planners have to look for ways to improve cities that are already built. But for some cities, growth has been planned from the beginning. The city planners have done this so that the settlement will look pleasant and work well.

In 1967 the country of Belize (then called British Honduras) began to build a new capital city. The old capital city, called Belize, was located on the coast. It was often hit by bad tropical storms called hurricanes. These hurricanes killed many people and destroyed many parts of the city. Belize was built on very low land and suffered from floods. The old capital was also very overcrowded. It could not grow any more because it was surrounded by mangrove swamps. Also, many homes were made of wood. This was a fire hazard. Fig. 2.20 shows the old capital city.

1 Imagine you are a city planner. Your aim is to find a place to build a new capital city which will not have the problems of the old capital.

2 Look at Fig. 2.21 carefully. It shows five possible sites A, B, C, D and E for the country's new capital city. Study each possible site in turn. As you do this think about these things:
  (i) communications
  (ii) flood risk
 (iii) hurricanes
 (iv) distance from other towns
  (v) fresh water supply.

3 Write a short report which:
  (i) states the site you have chosen
  (ii) explains why you have chosen the site.

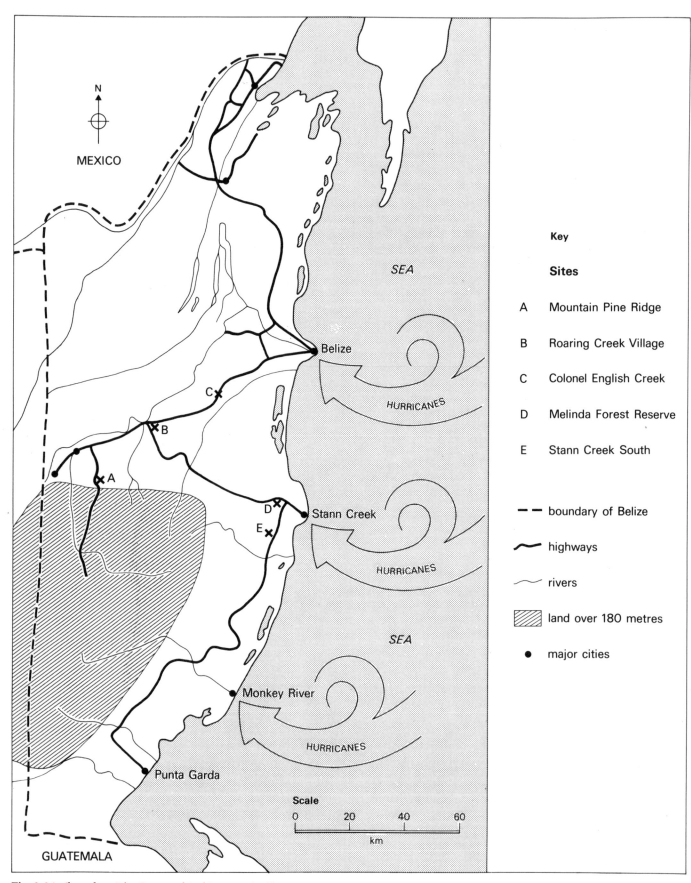

Key

Sites

A   Mountain Pine Ridge

B   Roaring Creek Village

C   Colonel English Creek

D   Melinda Forest Reserve

E   Stann Creek South

- - -   boundary of Belize

⌒   highways

⌒   rivers

▨   land over 180 metres

●   major cities

MEXICO

SEA

HURRICANES

Belize

C

B

A

D

Stann Creek

E

HURRICANES

SEA

Monkey River

HURRICANES

Punta Garda

GUATEMALA

Scale

0   20   40   60

km

Fig. 2.21 (based on *The Geographical Review,* **April 1973)**

The site the city planners chose for the new capital is described below. Which of the sites A, B, C, D or E do you think is described in their report?

These are some of the things the planners wrote:

'The chosen site is located 50 km from the coast. It is safe from direct hurricane damage. Being sixty metres above sea level the site is unlikely to flood. It has a good supply of fresh drinking water from the Belize River. It can be easily reached as it is at the junction of two main highways. It is an equal distance from the two large cities of Belize and Stann Creek. The city will be called Belmopan'.

4 Compare this with your own report. How far do you agree or disagree with their choice?

5 Looking inside Belmopan we see that the buildings and facilities form an interesting pattern on the ground (see Fig. 2.22).

(i) Using what you have learnt in this book explain why the different types of land use are divided by areas of open space.

(ii) Give two reasons to explain why the industrial area is located where it is.

(iii) Explain the layout of major roads.

Topolis

This exercise looks at the development of one form of land use inside a city. You and seven others in your class will work together as a planning group. You have all been asked by the City Corporation of Topolis to plan the growth of housing for the next fifteen years. The population of Topolis today is about 75 000. In fifteen years' time it is likely to be 95 000. Most of these extra people will have to live in houses that have to be built within the area shown in Fig. 2.23. Your aim is to choose seventy-five blocks for future housing development.

Fig. 2.22 Inside Belmopan (based on *The Geographical Review***, April 1973)**

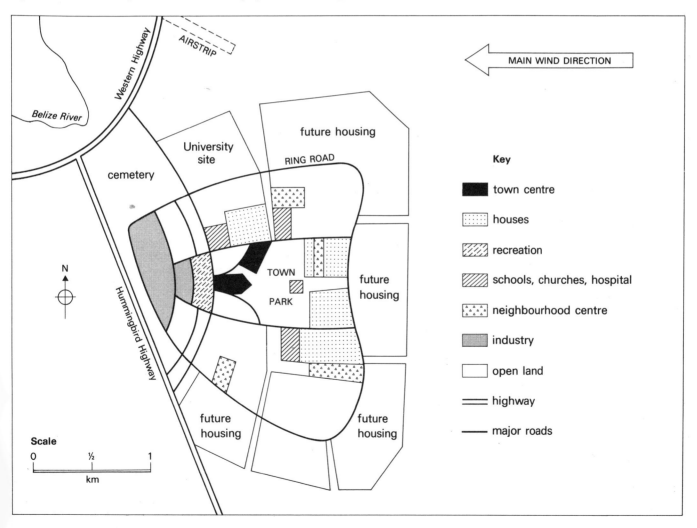

Fig. 2.23

TOPOLIS

What to do

1 For each planning group there are eight role cards. These are shown in Table 2.9. Read through this table carefully and decide who you want to be. This will be your role.

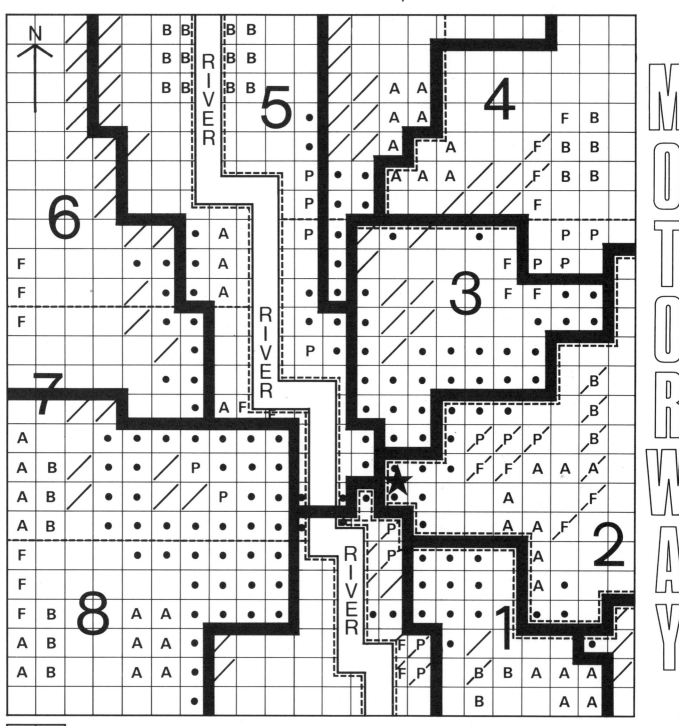

Scale:
= 1 square kilometre

Table 2.9

MR or MISS SWIFT

Houses built along existing main roads, marked on the base map by thick black lines, means that people can get to the houses very easily. In other words being next to existing main roads ENCOURAGES housing development.

If a new house is built next to an existing main road the occupier is generally able to travel into the city easily for shopping or to get to work. Usually the occupier has only a short walk to a bus stop to catch a bus into the city.

You should recommend that: THE BLOCKS THAT ARE NEXT TO EXISTING MAIN ROADS ARE THE BEST BLOCKS FOR HOUSE BUILDING.

MR or MISS GRIMES

Sewage works, noisy factories, large new roads, railway tracks and so on, are things which people generally do not want to live near. They may be said to *pollute* the area. You must let your friends know that these things DISCOURAGE housing development.

On the base map you can see a number of large letters 'P'. These mean that the block is influenced by certain '*polluting*' factors.

You should argue that, given a choice, nobody is really going to want to live near to these 'polluting' factors. In other words you should recommend that: HOUSES SHOULD BE BUILT AS FAR AWAY AS POSSIBLE FROM THE BLOCKS WITH THE LETTER P IN THEM.

MR or MISS WOODS

Many people prefer to buy houses near to areas of natural beauty. Many people are likely to live in houses built in areas overlooking beautiful hills, the river, green fields or areas that are not built-up. In other words being close to areas of natural beauty ENCOURAGES housing development.

On the base map you can see a number of large letters B. These mean that the blocks have great natural beauty.

House building *in* the blocks marked with a letter B should be VERY ACTIVELY DISCOURAGED.

You should recommend that: THE BLOCKS NEXT TO THOSE BLOCKS WITH THE LETTER B IN THEM ARE THE BEST BLOCKS FOR HOUSE BUILDING.

MR or MISS PARKS

When deciding which are the best blocks in which to build houses, you must let your friends know that there are other people, besides house builders, who might want to use these blocks. For example some people might want to build a factory or a recreation centre where your friends want to build their houses. You must argue that demand by people, other than house builders, for the block, DISCOURAGES housing development.

On the base map you can see a number of large letters A. These mean that other people, besides house builders, want to use that block.

You should recommend that: THE BLOCKS WITHOUT THE LETTER A IN THEM ARE THE BEST BLOCKS FOR HOUSE BUILDING.

MR or MISS FISHER

After a long period of heavy rain, the whole of the river shown on the base map is likely to spill over its banks and flood the blocks on either side. During winter time large areas near the river become marshy and boggy. You must let your friends know that being near to the river DISCOURAGES housing development.

On the base map you can see a number of large letters 'F'. These mean that not only the blocks on either side of the river, but also these marked blocks are likely to be flooded or become boggy after a long period of rain. You should argue that, given a choice, people are not going to want to live in these blocks.

You should recommend that: THE BLOCKS FURTHEST AWAY FROM THE BIG RIVER AND THE BLOCKS WITHOUT THE LETTER F IN THEM, ARE THE BEST BLOCKS FOR HOUSING DEVELOPMENT.

MR or MISS HOUSEMAN

Generally houses built next to already built-up areas, marked on the base map by a black dot, are more desirable than houses that are built away from built-up areas. In other words, being next to existing built-up areas ENCOURAGES housing development.

If a new house is built next to existing houses, it is likely to be near to many facilities which we need. For example, roads to help us travel easily from place to place, gas and electricity supplies to keep us warm and cook our food, corner shops, schools and so on.

You should recommend that: THE BLOCKS THAT ARE NEXT TO EXISTING BUILT-UP AREAS ARE THE BEST BLOCKS FOR HOUSE BUILDING.

MR or MISS CLOSE

Generally people who buy houses want to be as close to the city centre as possible, for shopping and working. You must let your friends know that being near to the city centre of Topolis ENCOURAGES housing development.

On the base map you can see a black star. This marks the centre of Topolis. You should recommend that: THE BLOCKS THAT ARE CLOSEST TO THE CITY CENTRE ARE THE BEST BLOCKS FOR HOUSE BUILDING.

MR or MISS LANE

The population of Topolis is going to increase by 20 000 people. There will not be enough work in the city for all these extra people. So, many of these extra people are going to have to travel to a nearby big city for work. There is a motorway which joins Topolis to this big city. You must let your friends know that being close to the motorway ENCOURAGES housing development.

On the base map you can see that the motorway is found on the eastern side of Topolis and lies in a north–south direction. When you discuss zones 1–8 you should argue that the best blocks for house building are those in the EAST of the city.

You should recommend that: THE BLOCKS THAT ARE CLOSEST TO THE MOTORWAY ARE THE BEST BLOCKS FOR HOUSING DEVELOPMENT.

55

2 Study the map of Topolis (Fig. 2.23). Notice that:
(i) the map is divided into eight development zones
(ii) the roads (thick black lines) and the river are drawn on a grid pattern
(iii) the black dots show the extent of the built up land in Topolis today
(iv) the map is also divided into a number of small blocks. Houses can be built in any block that does not have a black dot in it.
(v) some blocks have letters in them. A letter:
P means that the block is affected by some form of pollution.
F means that the block is liable to flood at certain times of the year.
A means that the block is demanded for non-house building (alternative) purposes.
B means that the block is an area of great natural beauty.
(vi) the thin diagonal black line in some blocks represents those blocks which Topolis Corporation suggest are the best places for future houses. You may agree or disagree with their suggestions.
(vii) a star marks the centre of the city.

3 Planning where to build houses is to be in three rounds, each round representing a five year period.
(i) Each zone is to be taken in turn. When every development zone has been considered once, housing development will equal one five year period.
(ii) Each zone will be considered three times. This will equal fifteen years of housing development in Topolis.
(iii) You should plan to develop twenty-five blocks every five years. Lack of money means you cannot develop more than this in any one five year period. Demand for houses means that you cannot develop less than twenty-five blocks in any five year plan.
(iv) You do not have to build in every zone but consider the Corporation's suggestions first, each time you enter a new zone.
(v) You must always remember the role you are playing.
Although your role card gives you some information to help you in your discussions with others in your planning group, you will need to think of some more arguments for yourself.

4 After discussing the possibilities for housing development in each zone, complete your 'decision sheet'. This sheet will help you keep a record of what happens zone by zone, and round by round. On your decision sheet you must try to make a summary of
(i) where you as a planning group have decided to build. You could also place a piece of tracing paper over Fig. 2.23 and with different colours representing each round, record on your tracing paper where you plan to build. Or
(ii) why you have decided not to build in that zone
(iii) the reasons why you agree or disagree with the group's decision.
As a group you must work out how you intend to make decisions in order to plan enough houses for the growing population of Topolis.

Decision sheet

ZONE . . .		ROUND . . .
1 Where we plan to build in this development zone		
2 Why we have decided not to build in this development zone		
3 Reasons why I agree with the group's decision		
4 Reasons why I disagree with the group's decision		

Follow-up work

After completing three rounds:
1 Prepare a base map on which you show all the blocks you plan to develop for houses over the next fifteen years. Compare your map with others in your class.
2 Prepare a planning summary to read to the class. In the summary state clearly:
(i) some of the important and interesting arguments put forward by members of your group
(ii) whether any overall plan was behind your group's decisions. e.g. that in Round 2 (6–10 years time) development will be restricted to areas on the west bank of the river. Say how you justified your overall plans
(iii) how your group finally decided which blocks to develop once the discussion about each zone had taken place.

What can be done?

Living in settlements has many advantages. Depending on their population, settlements can support shops, factories and many kinds of leisure pursuits. But settlements also have their problems. One such problem is that people are wanting more and better living space for themselves and their families, bigger houses and gardens for example. More space is needed for work. More space for workers and machines. More space for shops, roads and schools. It is in the inner areas of some large towns and cities that the problems of living and working are most serious.

1 Study Figs. 2.24 and 2.25 carefully. They show some of the major problems the planners have to solve in some inner areas of large settlements. Think back to the work you have done in this book. Now try to make a list of some of the causes of each problem.

Fig. 2.24 Major problems in some inner city areas: (a) Empty and under-used land *(above)* **(b) Empty and under-used buildings** *(bottom left)* **(c) Hold-ups of people, vehicles and goods** *(bottom right)*

Fig. 2.25 Poor housing

In order to try to solve some of these problems every County Council in England and Wales is required, by law, to make a Structure Plan. A Structure Plan is a land development plan. It describes what needs to be done in the County and shows how the planners hope to do it. In writing a plan County Councils have to get the views of a large number of people. The general public is given a chance to ask questions about it and to make their own suggestions about land development.

Some planners believe that the starting point for dealing with the problems of inner city areas is to find out what the people who live there want. For example they try to find out what kind of dwelling people want as their home; they find out what sort of surroundings people like. They ask questions to find out whether people want a home near to local shops and some open space. If they want to be near a public transport route, a Primary School, a Church or a Community Centre. Planners also have to find out whether all these need to be in a 'green setting'.

2 Study Fig. 2.26. It shows some ways of improving life in inner city areas.

3 Look at Table 2.10. Your class has been asked to prepare an 'Inner Area Development Plan'. Your class is to be divided into seven groups. You are to choose to belong to one of these groups.

4 Each group needs to:
(i) study Figs 2.24, 2.25 and 2.26
(ii) try to find out more about inner area

Table 2.10

Group name	Group responsible for	Group leader
1 Housing	New houses. Letting, repairing and maintaining existing houses. Rehousing people.	Director of Housing
2 Engineers	Building and caring for roads, pavements, street lighting, cleaning, rubbish collection, traffic control and road safety.	Chief City Engineer
3 Estate and Property	Buying land for the city council. Managing and caring for public buildings e.g. Libraries.	Chief Surveyor
4 Social Service	The well being of the family, children, young people, elderly and handicapped.	Director of Social Services
5 Medical	Clinics, hospitals, environmental health and spotting unfit homes.	Medical Officer of Health
6 Education	Schools, Further Education, school meals, youth clubs and community services.	Director of Education
7 Treasury	Mortgages, loans of money. House rents.	City Treasurer

development plans. Many large cities in the UK have inner area development plans. Discuss with your teacher the possibility of writing to a city planning officer, asking for information about their inner area development plan

(iii) write a report. Give it a suitable title. This will be put with other group reports to form a class development plan called 'Inner City Action'. In your group report you need to:

(a) include an overall group aim.

(b) make a list of group suggestions, in an order of importance, which aim to help improve life in inner city areas.

(c) explain how each of your suggestions might do this.

(d) illustrate some of your suggestions with pictures and drawings for a class display.

5 Put all the group reports and illustrations together. Your teacher could act as Chief Planning Officer and organise the overall display.

6 Each group leader is to describe and explain his group report to the rest of the class.

Fig. 2.26 Some ways of improving life in inner city areas

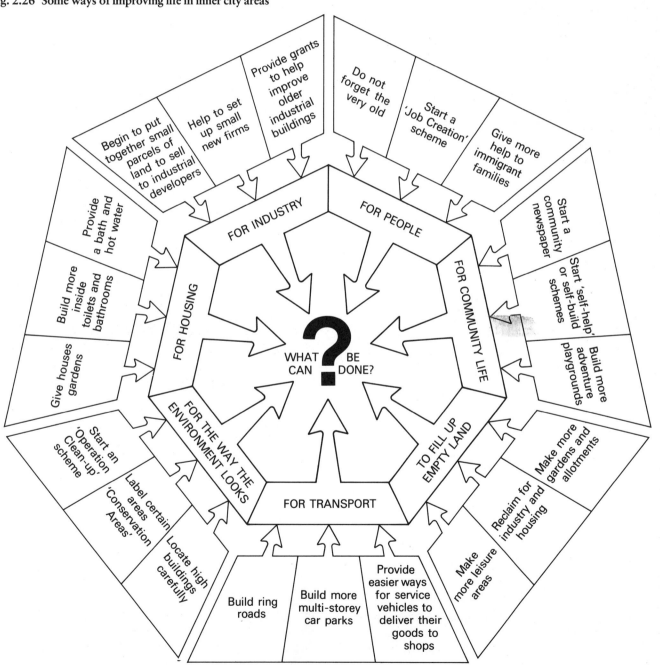

What has been done

The name Singapore comes from two old Indian
words, *Singa* (Lion) and *Pura* (City). Legend has it that
a prince once landed in Tumasek (Sea Town) and saw a
beast which he thought was a lion. He promptly
renamed the place Singa Pura.

Today Singapore has changed from an island of
fishing villages to one of the busiest ports in the world.
With a population of 2.4 million people and another 1
million visitors each year, Singapore needs to plan and
redevelop her scarce land very carefully. Land
shortages have meant that new buildings grow
skywards rather than spread out over the land.
Singapore is a busy, bustling island of activity and
change in South-East Asia.

1 Study Fig. 2.27 carefully. It shows two different
areas before and after redevelopment.

2 Describe the problems shown in each photo
before redevelopment (you may care to refer back to
Figs. 2.24 and 2.25 to help you do this).

3 Study each photo which shows the
redevelopment that has been taking place in each area.
How would you argue that redevelopment solves some
old urban problems but may cause new ones?

Fig. 2.27 Redevelopment in Singapore.
(a) Middle Road before *(above left)* and after *(bottom left)*
redevelopment.
(b) Chin Swee Road before *(above)* and after *(below)*
redevelopment.

Acknowledgements

The authors wish to thank the students and staff of Worcester College of Higher Education, and a large number of Middle and Secondary school teachers who have made many helpful and constructive comments on each book. Special thanks go to Deborah Kennedy, Margaret Hawkesworth, Tony Matthews, Kevin Wilbur and David Brockie for the ideas and materials they have offered. The authors would also like to thank Bill Kelly for his help and encouragement and David Oliver who has been a great source of inspiration.

The authors and publishers wish to acknowledge the following photograph sources:

Australian Information Service p. 2 top;   Barnabys Picture Library p. 58;   Basildon Development Corporation p. 39 bottom;   Birmingham City Corporation p. 28;   Jim Brownbill pp. 34 centre left and bottom, 42 bottom;   J. Allan Cash Ltd pp. 7 top left, 8 top, 45 top left, right, bottom left; An Esso Photograph p. 29 bottom left;   F.A.O. Photo by G De Sabatino pp. 21 bottom, 22 top, bottom, left and right;   F.A.O. Photo by T Page p. 21 top left, top right;   F.A.O. Photo by S Baron p. 22 centre left;   Ford of Britain p. 7 top right;   Forestry Commission p. 43 bottom;   Gatwick Airport Authorities p. 42 top;   Government of Alberta, Canada p. 26;   Greater London Council p. 29 top right;   Keystone Press Agency Ltd. pp. 7 bottom, 48, 49, 50, 57 top and bottom left;   Middle East Archives p. 7 centre; Oxfam p. 21 centre;   Popperfoto pp. 45 bottom right, 51, 57 bottom right; Scottish Tourist Board p. 8 bottom;   Singapore Urban Redevelopment Authority p. 59;   Vauxhall Motors Ltd. p. 43 top. *Cover*: Alan Hutchinson Library.